THEY WERE THERE

THEY WERE THERE

Two Series of Lenten Monologs

Roy Barlag
Richard Andersen

Publishing House
St. Louis

Concordia Publishing House, St. Louis, Missouri

Manufactured in the United States of America

Library of Congress Cataloging in Publication Data

Barlag, Roy, 1916-
They were there.

1. Lenten sermons. 2. Lutheran Church—Sermons.
3. Sermons, American. I. Andersen, Richard, 1931-
joint author. II. Title.
BV4277.B315 252'.62 77-13189
ISBN 0-570-03769-7

CONTENTS

JUDAS

I was born in the town of Kerioth. That is why you refer to me as Judas Iscariot, to distinguish me from the other Judas, who was also one of the original 12 apostles.

You think you know me, don't you? You have already judged me, even before you have heard me out. You can't even speak my name without making it sound like a dirty word. Your artists make me look like the devil himself. But what do you really know of me, apart from the fact that I betrayed Jesus to those who then crucified Him? Well, let me tell you more. It may do you some good to learn that I was not a whole lot different from any of you who despise me.

Don't get me wrong. I'm not going to try to justify myself for what I did. I've been judged and condemned by a wiser judge than any of you. I'm not crying "Foul!" nor asking for a retrial. I think you should understand me, however, for it will be only by the grace of God if you wind up any differently than I did.

You may not want to name your children after me, but I can assure you that the name Judas was once an honorable name, as respectable as that of Peter, James, John, or any of the others. Judas is just another form of the name Judah, the tribe from which Jesus was born. One of Jesus' ancestors was named Judas. And one of the greatest folk heroes of my people was Judas Maccabeus, a great leader of the Jews whose exploits are still celebrated every year in the religious festival of Hannukuh. I don't understand how my one act of betrayal could do so much damage to the honorable name of Judas!

Do you think I was always a traitor? Listen, for three years I was a follower of Jesus. Do you understand? I followed Him, for three years, more closely perhaps than some of you who claim to be His followers now. I didn't start out with the intention of betraying Him.

I suppose you wonder what my motives were in becoming a disciple of Jesus, considering how it all ended. I'm not sure that I myself fully understand what my original motives were—

probably mixed. But while we're on the subject, try analyzing your own motivation sometime. You might be in for an embarrassing revelation, if you're honest with yourself. Do you think everyone who answers the call of Jesus to follow Him does so with motives that are always one hundred percent pure? Take James and John for example, two of Jesus' special favorites. They wanted the positions of highest importance when Jesus established His kingdom. They even had their mother try to influence Jesus to grant their proud and selfish request. And do you think the rest of the apostles were any better? They were angry at James and John only because they themselves were vying for the same positions.

Well, whatever their motives—or mine—may have been, we heard the Lord say: "If any man will come after Me, let him deny himself!" That wasn't going to be easy, and we knew it. Yet we did forsake everything, leaving homes and jobs to follow Jesus. I was one of that select circle of apostles.

Don't forget that I was an accepted member of the Twelve. They picked me to be the treasurer of the group. You must admit that they trusted me during those three years of our association, or they wouldn't have let me handle the money. Even after I had secretly made a deal with the chief priests, they still trusted me. When Jesus, on the night before He died, announced to us that one of us would betray Him, the others did not suspect me. They all began to search their own hearts, and each asked, "Lord, is it I?" I was still considered to be as loyal a friend of Jesus as any of them.

Jesus had accepted me too. He chose me as one of His 12 disciples, and in that capacity I served Him for three years at least as faithfully as the others. And Jesus loved me too, even when He knew that I had already turned my back on Him and betrayed Him.

Don't get the idea that just because Jesus once said, "One of you is devilish!" in a prophetic reference to me, that this means He didn't love me and that I was all bad. He was just as harsh in His criticism of Peter, whom He once called "Satan" to his face. Both instances were acts of love—warnings—as loving as the tears He shed over the inhabitants of Jerusalem who rejected Him.

How then, you ask, did I become disloyal enough to betray Jesus to His enemies? Well, as I've said, I didn't start out with that idea in mind. And I didn't get the idea all of a sudden, either. It was a gradual development, and I'm telling you this so that you can see how easily it could happen to you too.

Even now, in looking back, I can put my finger on any one thing that led to my betrayal of Jesus. It's true that I had a wrong conception of the kind of Messiah Jesus was to be. I knew He was to be a liberator, one who would set His people free. But I was thinking more in terms of a political Messiah, who would rid us of the Roman army of occupation.

I wasn't alone in my misconception. The others in our group felt pretty much the same way—with the possible exception of Levi, or Matthew, as you call him. He had worked as a tax collector for Rome and was of the opinion that we should accept Roman rule and make the best of a bad situation by collaborating with the enemy. Matthew and Simon Zelotes, who was at the opposite end of the political spectrum, used to have some hot arguments on the subject when they thought Jesus wasn't listening.

You have to understand that nearly all of my people had come to think of the promised Messiah as one who would come to reestablish a free and independent kingdom of the Jews. That idea dated back about 500 years to the time of our nation's captivity in Babylon, when all that the exiles could think of was freedom and a return to their homeland.

Anyway, as it became more and more apparent that Jesus had no such political aspirations or objectives in mind, I began to lose interest in Him. If only I had more carefully studied the Scriptures, especially the prophecies of Isaiah, I might not have been so misled by my wishful thinking.

In a way I felt like something of an outsider among the disciples. They all came from the northern province of Galilee, where Jesus had grown to manhood. My hometown of Kerioth was at the opposite end of the kingdom. The others used to tease me about my accent, so different from theirs, and I guess I secretly resented it; although as I said before, they showed their acceptance of me by making me treasurer of the group.

John has said that I was a thief and greedy. He might have been more charitable in his judgment if he'd had the responsibility of my job. A lot he knew about finances! All he could comprehend was the fishing business. I at least understood the value of money. If I took anything from the common treasury, it was only to compensate for expenses incurred and in lieu of the salary I didn't get. Once, the others stood around and watched approvingly while Mary of Bethany wasted a pound of expensive ointment anointing Jesus' feet. I pointed out that it could have been sold and put to better use. It really hurt my feelings when Jesus sided with the others and defended Mary's wasteful act as proper under the circumstances.

It also annoyed me very much that Jesus gave preferential treatment to a few of the apostles—especially to that big, blustering braggart, Simon Peter, and his fishing partners, James and John. You say I was jealous? Maybe so.

These are some of the things that led up to that night when I secretly approached Jesus' enemies, the chief priests, and offered to tell them where they could find Jesus and arrest Him when He was not surrounded by a crowd of people sympathetic to Him. As you know, they gave me 30 pieces of silver for the information, on the condition that I myself lead them to the place.

I don't remember what I planned to do with the money. At the time I wasn't even sure that I would go through with it. I was still with Jesus and the others in the upper room where we celebrated the Passover festival together. It was the most miserable festival in my life, suspecting as I did that Jesus knew exactly what was in my heart and mind. And when He quietly informed me that He did indeed know, and told me to hurry up and get it over with, I couldn't stand it any longer. I rushed out where the darkness of the night matched the gloom in my soul.

It was a late hour to be contacting the priests, but when I told them where Jesus and the others would be going, Caiaphas immediately dispatched a hastily assembled posse to the Garden of Gethsemane on the Mount of Olives east of Jerusalem with authority to arrest Jesus and bring Him back to the high priest's palace. I went along to make certain that they came back with the right man.

You'll understand, I'm sure, if I don't dwell on the events in the Garden of Gethsemane. That's the one brief moment of my life with which you are already most familiar anyway. Suffice it to say there was only bitterness in my heart when I put the finger on Jesus with the prearranged signal to the priest's men. Jesus spoke gently to me. It would have been easier to bear had He struck me or spoken harshly. I avoided His eyes and left immediately.

You know, even then I didn't fully realize the seriousness of my betrayal. If Jesus had come to Jerusalem to be arrested and put to death, as He had said, then what difference did it make who betrayed Him? If not I, it would have been someone else. Of course, now I know that though it made no difference where Jesus was concerned, it made all the difference in the world to me. I had now turned my back on Christ once and for all. All the hopes I had built up in three years of discipleship had vanished.

I didn't actually think about it, but I may have felt that Jesus could escape any time He wanted to. He had demonstrated His power to do this many times before. Besides, I underestimated the priests. I didn't see how they could actually sentence Him to death, for I knew that Jesus had done nothing wrong.

However, when I saw that Jesus was quickly condemned by the Sanhedrin, and was led to the court of Pilate for sentencing, I tried to undo what was done, by offering to return the 30 pieces of silver if the priests would release Jesus. But they wouldn't even listen, and I felt I had now reached the point of no return. In despair I ended my own life.

That's my story. Now which of you can honestly say that you haven't more than once set foot on the path away from Christ—a path that for me led to destruction? You and I are not so very different. A little ignorance of the Scriptures and of the real nature of Christ's kingdom, a little disappointment in Him, a little too much love of money, a little envy and jealousy, a bit of unjustifiable anger—and you could be well on the road to becoming another Judas.

CAIAPHAS

Caiaphas is my name. I'm the high priest here in Jerusalem. Well, actually my father-in-law Annas is still regarded by the people as their high priest—which he was for many years. But Annas is a stubborn old fool, and when the Romans conquered our land and sent their troops to keep order in Jerusalem, Annas wasn't clever enough to keep out of trouble with the Roman government. Consequently he was kicked out of office about 15 years ago, and I landed the job. I don't like to brag, but I have not only managed to get along with the Romans; I even know how to manipulate them, twist them around my finger, to get what I want.

Take Pontius Pilate for example. He's the Roman governor of Judea. When we had Jesus of Nazareth, a self-styled Messiah, brought before Pilate for sentencing a little over a month ago, Pilate had every intention of letting Jesus go free. After all the trouble we had gone through, to catch Jesus and bring Him to trial, I wasn't about to let Him get away. So I just put the pressure on Pilate and finally got what I wanted. The Romans authorized and carried out a sentence of death on Jesus. He was taken to a hill outside of Jerusalem and crucified.

But I'm getting ahead of my story. Let me tell you how it happened. It all began about three years ago. Down along the Jordan River, near the north end of the Dead Sea, not too far from here, a wild man by the name of John started causing a lot of excitement by preaching to the crowds that came out there to see him. Even though he lived pretty much of a hermit's life out in the desert, where he existed on locusts and wild honey for food, preaching must have come easily to him, for he was the son of a priest by the name of Zacharias.

The thing that annoyed me was that John was drawing such crowds out of the city. Some of the people who would normally have been spending their money at the temple in Jerusalem, where I'm high priest, were going out to listen to him instead. His message was nearly always the same: They were sinners and should repent, because the time for the coming of the Messiah was at hand.

We sent out a delegation once to check up on him, and he was very sarcastic, calling our men some bad names and saying that *we* were all sinners and should repent. We asked him if he were claiming to be the Messiah or some great prophet. He said No, but that the Messiah would soon appear. That's about when this Jesus of Nazareth came to our attention. When He came out to the Jordan to be baptized, John said of Him: "Behold, the Lamb of God, who takes away the sin of the world!"

Anyway, after that the Sanhedrin—that's the Supreme Court, of which I'm the chief justice—began to be more concerned about the activity of Jesus than of John. Some of John's followers left him and began to follow Jesus, and now the Nazarene began posing an even greater threat to our authority. Besides, we didn't have to worry about John for long. He got himself into hot water with Herod Antipas, the ruler of the province of Galilee. He accused Herod of adultery for messing around with his brother Philip's wife, and after a while Herod celebrated his birthday by having John's head cut off.

Then this Jesus really began to be a nuisance. He was all over the place, preaching to crowds here in Jerusalem, and way up around the Sea of Tiberias in Galilee, and in Perea on the east side of the Jordan River. He even went through Samaria, where no self-respecting Jew would go, because we and the Samaritans don't get along.

They say He performed miracles wherever He went—maybe so. Some of the things He taught were an aggravation to us. He spoke of angels, and of a life after death, which I and my fellow Sadducees think is a lot of bunk. But we were used to that kind of talk, because the Pharisees on our council also held those beliefs. However, Jesus aggravated the Pharisees too, by ignoring some of the traditions they hold sacred.

The upshot of it all was that Jesus was becoming too important to the people for us to ignore. People were starting to listen to Him instead of listening to us, their religious leaders. Jesus began to be the kind of opposition and competition to us that had to be stopped before it went too far.

Do you know He actually had the gall to chase the sellers of cattle and sheep off the temple premises with a whip and to dump over the tables of the money-changers?! He shouted at them: "My house shall be called a house of prayer, but you have made it a den of thieves!" *His* house! Hmph! I should tell you that the sale of sacrificial animals and the money-changing in the temple is a mighty profitable business, especially at Passover time, when we've got a lot of people in town who have come a long way for the festival and need to exchange their foreign currency and buy their sacrifices here. That Jesus was really putting a crimp in our sales.

So we took swift action, calling together the 70 members of the Sanhedrin to discuss the situation. You know, we Sadducees on the council don't usually get along too well with the Pharisees, but on this issue we quickly agreed that something had to be done about Jesus of Nazareth.

However, when it comes to decisive action, the council, I'm sorry to say, is a bunch of ninnies. They didn't know what to do, so I took charge. "You fools!" I told them, "can't you see that for the good of the people this man Jesus must die?" They agreed, and from there on it was all cut and dried.

We paid one of Jesus' followers, a greedy fellow by the name of Judas, 30 pieces of silver to tell us where we could catch the Nazarene without a public ruckus. It was easy. About midnight on the Thursday before our Passover festival we grabbed Him in the Garden of Gethsemane east of town. Except for a bit of a struggle with one big fellow called Simon Peter, there was no resistance.

When Jesus was brought into my courtroom, after a preliminary hearing by my father-in-law Annas, we paid some men to give false testimony against Jesus. But those stupid liars gave conflicting testimony, which was useless. So once again I had to do it all by myself. I asked the Nazarene to say under oath whether He was the Christ, the Son of God; and when He said He was, we had Him dead to rights on a charge of blasphemy, that is, of dishonoring God by claiming to be God's Son.

The verdict was guilty, and I quickly pronounced the sentence of death. The trouble was that though our Sanhedrin can find a person deserving of death, we aren't allowed to carry out the execution. That has to be approved and carried out by the Romans. And so we took Jesus under guard to the Roman governor's palace, where we roused Pilate about six o'clock in the morning and told him what we wanted.

If I hadn't been on my toes, some of my naive colleagues would simply have said that we'd found Jesus guilty of blasphemy. Can you imagine Pilate's reaction if we had said, "He's guilty of blasphemy"?! He'd have laughed at us! "That's a religious problem," he'd have said, "a matter of theology, and no concern of mine." He'd have dismissed the case then and there, and we'd have been right back where we started.

Of course I was too smart to make a blunder like that. "He's an enemy of Caesar!" I said, "a troublemaker among the people, who claims to be our king." Can you imagine Pilate trying to ignore those charges? The way he acted, I don't think he believed them. He probably doubted that we would turn over to him an enemy of the Roman government, when we ourselves are not exactly wild about Caesar and his high and mighty governors.

But as I said, I know how to manipulate these Roman dogs. Just one little remark to the effect that anyone who'd let Jesus go free is no friend of Caesar was all it took to make Pilate knuckle under and order the execution.

So now He's dead—your Lord Jesus Christ. You'd think that now I could rest easy, with a little peace of mind for a change. But no, if anything, matters are getting worse. I just don't seem to have the hold on the people that I used to. They aren't satisfied just to bring their offerings to the temple and be done with it. They're starting to ask questions about just what the prophets did say concerning the promised Messiah, and about some of the things Jesus said and did. There are even a couple of members of the Sanhedrin, like that old Pharisee Gamaliel, who are beginning to suggest that maybe it was a mistake to put Jesus out of the way. The Nazarene is as much of a burden to me now as when He was alive.

Or *is* He alive? His body was never found after it disappeared from the tomb. Rumors have it that Jesus' followers have seen Him alive. I must be going out of my mind, for I'm almost beginning to believe it myself. I know that some strange and scary things happened on the day Jesus died. And the Roman officer in charge of the crucifixion is said to believe that Jesus was everything He claimed to be.

One thing is sure—we're going to have to put a muzzle on Jesus' disciples. They're going around again, talking about a resurrection. I don't know where they get the nerve to keep speaking of Jesus as their risen Lord. They just won't shut their mouths. They aren't the same scared rabbits they were. Things aren't the same anymore, since Jesus appeared on the scene.

Note: In A.D. 36 Caiaphas, the "manipulator," was deposed by the Romans.

PILATE

Pontius Pilate is my name. As the Roman governor of Judea, representative of Emperor Tiberius Caesar, I was the one who authorized the crucifixion of Jesus of Nazareth. But why should I introduce myself? You already know me. You Christians mention my name every time you recite your creed, in which you state that your Jesus suffered and was crucified under my jurisdiction.

I think you are passing the buck when you put all the blame for Jesus' death on my shoulders. What about His own people, who brought Him to me in the first place, demanding that I have Him crucified? And what about yourselves? Haven't I heard you sing in the words of one of your hymns: "Ah, I also and my sin wrought Thy deep affliction; This indeed the cause hath been of Thy crucifixion"?! If you believe that Jesus died on account of your sins, then why don't you honestly face up to your share of the guilt, instead of laying it all on me?

I know what I did was wrong. You don't need to keep reminding me. I have not had a decent night's sleep since it happened. On that day—the day you refer to as Good Friday—it all started early. I was sound asleep in my palace when they arrived. It must have been about five in the morning. How would you like to be awakened by a mob of fanatics screaming and shouting outside your house? Their leaders were some very important religious dignitaries who insisted on bringing a man into the courtroom for immediate trial.

I washed the sleep out of my eyes and let them in with their prisoner. As it turned out, they had been up all night, prejudging the case. They didn't want me to try the case, as much as they wanted me to just rubber-stamp their own conviction and sentence Jesus to death.

When I wanted to know what it was all about, they sarcastically said, "If He weren't a criminal, we wouldn't have brought Him to you!" How I hated them for their arrogance! They never did learn to accept their place as a conquered nation under Roman rule and authority. They showed me no respect.

But the feeling was mutual. I despised them as much as they did me, and I could be as sarcastic as they. So I said, "Take Him and judge Him according to your own law." That made them squirm, because I knew and they knew that they didn't have the authority to impose the death penalty. If they were going to use me to satisfy their blood lust, I was determined at least to make them crawl and beg.

So they said, "This fellow Jesus is a troublemaker who has been telling the people not to pay taxes to Caesar, and saying that He Himself is Christ, a king."

I don't know what kind of fool they took me for. Pretending they were concerned about disloyalty to Caesar! They themselves were among the least loyal subjects of Caesar. If Jesus had been a real threat to the Roman government, they would have given Him their secret support instead of bringing Him to me demanding that He be crucified. The chief priests thought Jesus posed a threat all right, but to them as the spiritual leaders of their people; not to Rome.

I know I should have ended the farce right there, but you have to understand my position. They said Jesus claimed to be a king. That was a charge of treason. Whether I believed their charge or not, I had no choice but to examine Jesus. So I took Him to the courtroom and began my interrogation.

"Are You the King of the Jews?" I asked. I must say He didn't look like a king, standing there in chains, with the blood running from cuts on His face where they had hit Him. But He said, "Yes, I am a king!" and I must admit there was something regal about His bearing. However, He made it clear that His kingdom posed no threat to Caesar. He was some kind of religious Christ or Messiah. "I came into the world to bear witness to the truth," He said.

I couldn't take that seriously. "What is truth?" I asked. Tell me, do you know what truth is? Are you so sure of anything that you would stake your life or your reputation on it? There must be some of you who think as I do, that nothing is absolutely true. It's all relative.

But I do envy and admire the courage and peace of mind of those followers of Jesus who accept His Word as the absolute truth, who live and die believing they are God's own redeemed children through faith in Him. I've gone through life looking for something like that—something to believe in; looking in vain.

But let me continue. I knew that your Jesus was innocent of the charges brought against Him. I guess I knew it from the moment I first saw Him. And I did not really want Him crucified. I tried to set Him free, but the people wouldn't hear of it. They kept insisting that Jesus must die.

You don't understand how I could knowingly send an innocent man to his death? Don't be so sure you wouldn't have done the same thing in my position. Looking back, I wish I hadn't done it. The awful dreams, the torment of mind I've had since then! But I had no choice. The priests said that if I didn't sentence Jesus to death by crucifixion, they would report me to Caesar as one who let an enemy of the state go free. The emperor wouldn't even have taken time to investigate a charge like that. I'd have been put out of office in a moment, or perhaps even executed as a traitor. I couldn't take a chance on that. It was Jesus' life or mine. I couldn't afford to be fussy about whether my verdict was right or wrong. I had to save my own skin, didn't I?

Don't think I gave your Jesus up to His enemies without a struggle. Let me tell you how hard I tried to do the right thing. I had started a custom of releasing one Jewish prisoner from jail every year at Passover time. It kept the people pacified. They were a little easier to govern if I did them a small favor now and then. Anyway, I had a notorious criminal named Barabbas in prison at the time—a real bad character. So I told the people I'd let them pick either Jesus or Barabbas to be set free. I could hardly believe my ears when they shouted: "Release Barabbas! Crucify Jesus!"

Then I heard it mentioned that Jesus was from the province of Galilee, which was really out of my jurisdiction. King Herod was ruler over Galilee, and since he was in Jerusalem at the time, I sent Jesus over to him, thinking maybe I could get rid of the whole sticky mess. I should have known better. Herod just had a little fun at Jesus' expense and sent Him back to me for sentencing.

Then I had Jesus scourged. Have you ever seen a man scourged? No, I guess you haven't, and I hope you never do; for it's a sight to turn a strong man's stomach. We Romans use a whip with leather thongs that have bits of bone or metal tied to the ends. A scourging tears the flesh right off the victim's back. Thirty-nine lashes was all the law allowed. More than that would kill a man. Some died anyway.

Jesus was given the limit that the law allowed. Then, to add insult to injury, my soldiers pressed a crown of thorns into His head, beat Him, spat on Him, and mocked Him. Cruel? Yes, I know it was—terribly cruel. But don't you see? The people were screaming for Jesus' death, and I thought that if they saw Him after a scourging they'd have pity on Him, that their blood lust would be satisfied. But I underestimated the degree of their hatred.

So it finally came to this, that I turned Jesus over to them to be crucified, knowing full well that I was condemning an innocent man to death. I was wrong. I admit it. My wife, a good woman, warned me. She had a dream about Jesus which she took to be a sign from God. I wouldn't listen to what I regarded as the hysteria of an emotional woman. Now I'm the one who is tormented in my dreams and can find no peace.

But who are you to keep laying the guilt for the death of Jesus on me in your creed? You Christians say that Jesus died in atonement for your sins, don't you? Doesn't that make you as guilty as I am? You may not have driven the nails through His hands and feet with your own hands. But for that matter, neither did I. My soldiers carried out the gruesome task. But I, you, we are the cause.

O God, what can we do to remove the blood from our hands, the guilt from our soul? I took some water and washed my hands in full view of the mob and said, "I am innocent of the blood of this just man!" But I wasn't fooling them or myself. That attempt at self-justification didn't give me a moment's peace of mind.

One of my men, the officer in charge of the crucifixion detail, came back saying that he believes your Jesus is the Son of God. He said that Jesus cried out from the cross, "Father, forgive them!" I wonder if He meant even me. If I could believe that Jesus' death was in fact part of God's plan for the salvation of the world, that His death atoned even for my sins, that what your Jesus said about Himself is indeed the truth—then I could sleep in peace again, with a clear conscience for a change. But I don't know. . . . I don't know. . . .

Note: According to the historian Eusebius, Pontius Pilate was removed from office in A.D. 36 and banished to southern France, where he ultimately committed suicide.

HERODThe time: A.D. 36
The place: Spain

My name is Herod Antipas. I'm one of the four judges in whose courts Jesus of Nazareth was tried and sentenced to death by crucifixion. Annas, Caiaphas, and Pontius Pilate were the other three. Actually, they had a lot more to do with Jesus' trial than I did. My role in the affair was almost incidental. But you can judge for yourself.

Sometimes I get the blame for things I didn't do. That's probably because there is a whole family of us Herods, and several of us have gotten at least a mention in your Bible. So some people get us mixed up. No wonder—our family history is quite complex.

Just to set the record straight, let me give you a few details. I was named Antipas after my grandfather, who was made governor of Judea by the Roman emperor Julius Caesar about 40 years before the birth of Jesus. After Grandfather was murdered, my father, with the help of the Roman Mark Anthony, became king.

You know my father, who was called Herod the Great, as the man who killed the babies in Bethlehem in an unsuccessful attempt to destroy Jesus. He was more successful in eliminating some others whom he regarded as threats to his throne, including one of his ten wives, her brother and grandfather, and three of my brothers. As you may well imagine, there wasn't much love lost among us in our family. My father was such a hated man that he feared no one would grieve over his passing when he died. So he actually told my Aunt Salome to lock up some Jewish leaders in the tower of Jericho and execute them when he died, so there would be mourning in the land even if it wasn't for his death. Well, about a year or two after Jesus' birth my father died; the prisoners at Jericho were released, and no tears were shed over Herod the Great.

My brother Archelaus then became ruler of Judea, until he was deposed and replaced by the Roman governor Pontius Pilate. Meanwhile I became the ruler of the province of Galilee, where your Jesus grew up in the town of Nazareth. I didn't know anything about Him at the time. In fact, before I heard about Jesus, I heard about another Jewish prophet, one named John—John the Baptizer, they called him.

John was drawing such crowds and making such an impression on the people that my curiosity was aroused, so I sent for him and listened to what he had to say. You know, I really liked John. I admired his courage. He actually had the nerve to tell me to my face that I was a sinner and should repent. I didn't mind that so much, but then he began to get too personal and specific in his accusations.

My sister-in-law Herodias and I were having an affair. She left my brother Philip, and I divorced my wife, the daughter of King Aretas, so that Herodias and I could be married. John thought that was terrible! It sure wasn't any big deal compared to some of the things my father and brothers had done. But John called it SIN. If you think I was upset, you should have seen Herodias. She was furious and wanted John killed, but I just had him arrested and thrown into prison.

The matter came to a head on my birthday. We were having a big party, and for our entertainment my stepdaughter Salome performed a seductive dance. I was pretty drunk by then, and without considering what she might ask, I swore that I'd give her anything she wanted, up to half of my kingdom. Well, she and Herodias put their conniving heads together, and came up with the bloody idea that they wanted John the Baptist's head brought to them on a platter.

Drunk as I was, that still shook me up quite a bit, but I couldn't go back on my word in the presence of all our guests, so I gave the order to have John beheaded—and it was done.

I'll admit that my conscience bothered me a bit after that. When I first heard about Jesus of Nazareth going about the land, preaching, teaching, performing miracles, and calling people to repentance, it sounded so much like John that I started having nightmares and seeing ghosts, and I imagined that Jesus was John the Baptizer come back to life to haunt me.

I never actually met Jesus personally until He was on trial in Jerusalem and Pontius Pilate sent Him to me. Some of my friends had a run-in with Jesus once. Together with some Pharisees they contrived a tricky question in an attempt to trap Jesus into a statement that could be used against Him and weaken His popularity with the people; but Jesus saw through their trickery and the plan didn't work.

I was in Jerusalem at the time of Jesus' trial, staying at my father's castle there during the Jewish Passover, a great religious festival. The Sanhedrin, the Jewish high court, had already found Jesus guilty of blasphemy against God for calling Himself the Christ, the Son of God.

However, when they brought Him to Pilate, the Roman governor, they changed the charge against Jesus from blasphemy to one of treason and sedition, saying that Jesus was a threat to the Roman government since He claimed to be King of the Jews. Anyway, when Pilate learned that Jesus was from Galilee, he sent Him over to me since I was ruler of that province. I took it as a gesture of courtesy on Pilate's part and appreciated his consideration in the matter. Pilate and I had had our differences before, but after that we became friends.

Perhaps I should explain that I am not really a Jew, though you might say we are "kissing cousins." My father, Herod the Great, was an Edomite, a descendant of Jacob's twin brother Esau; and my mother was a Samaritan. Just for the sake of appearances I espoused the Jewish religion, leaning somewhat toward the religious views of the Sadducees; but actually, I couldn't have cared less about the religious charge of blasphemy brought against Jesus. And as far as the political charge of treason was concerned—that was just a big joke. No one seriously regarded Jesus and His followers as posing a threat to the Roman Empire.

If I had any opinion about the case at all, it was that Jesus was being framed by the religious leaders who regarded Him as a threat to their positions of power. But I was very glad for the chance to see Jesus. I had heard so many things about Him, especially about the miracles He is supposed to have performed. I was looking forward to a very entertaining evening and even invited some friends to a command performance of this miracle-worker. But I was disappointed. Not only did He refuse to display His bag of tricks; He actually refused even to speak to me—just stood there without saying a word when I interrogated Him.

Well, I can't tolerate that kind of insolence, so I let my

bodyguard poke fun at Him and ridicule Him by putting a royal robe on Him to mock His kingship. Then I sent Him back to Pilate without passing judgment. I'd had enough trouble with my Galilean subjects for executing the popular John. I wasn't about to get involved with another holy man.

Well, that's my story. I don't see why people seem to think of Herod as the epitome of all evil, unless of course they're still getting me mixed up with my father or my brother Archelaus, who was a violent and bloody ruler during his short reign. I like wine, women, and wild parties; and the only people I've killed are the ones who tried to deprive me of my pleasure.

That all happened a couple of years ago. Since then, it's been downhill with me. My former father-in-law, King Aretas, declared war on me for having divorced his daughter, and my army was wiped out. My friend Pilate was deposed and exiled to southern France. My friend Emperor Tiberius died, and his successor Caligula deposed me and exiled me to Spain. Here I've got nothing to look forward to in my old age but death. It's almost as though God—if there is a God—is punishing me. What was it John the Baptizer said so long ago? "Repent, for the kingdom of heaven is at hand!"

Note: There is nothing in history to indicate that Herod Antipas ever acknowledged his sins and repented. Some of us might detect within ourselves the same weaknesses that beset Herod, whose idea of living was the unrestrained indulgence of his physical appetites. Some people, like Herod, expect nothing of their religion and church than that it be entertaining.

Herod would not listen to John, and refused to take Jesus seriously. To us there comes again the call of John: "Repent!" and the invitation to behold Jesus as the Lamb of God that takes away the sin of the world—also our sin.

BARABBAS

The time: The day of Jesus' crucifixion
The place: At the edge of the crowd

I'm Barabbas. Call me "The People's Choice." I'm in a daze—hardly able to believe what has just happened to me. A few hours ago I was in chains in a dungeon, under sentence of death by crucifixion. Now, just like that, I have been set free. That man hanging there on the cross—the one in the middle—is suffering what I was scheduled to be suffering. It was Him or me. The matter was put to a vote by the people. One of us was to be turned loose, and the other would die. And the people almost unanimously picked me to be released. I had no idea I was so popular.

Well, actually my popularity had nothing to do with it. Nobody out there really likes me. They're afraid of me. Every time I look at them they turn their eyes away. If I try to talk to them they turn their backs on me and walk away. You're the first ones who have stopped to listen to me since Pilate's soldiers removed my chains, gave me a kick in the rear, and ordered me to leave town. Well, I'm leaving, but not until I satisfy my curiosity about that man Jesus, who's dying on that cross in my place; and not until I've figured out whom to thank for my freedom.

I sure don't aim to thank Pontius Pilate, the Roman governor. I'm not free because of the goodness of his heart. It's true that every year at the time of the Passover festival he has the practice of releasing one of the Jewish prisoners he has locked up. But he does that only because he's a smart politician. There are a lot of rebels who could stir up a fuss against Roman rule. And there are a lot of fanatics who would follow them in a rebellion against the Romans. So Pilate figures that the best way to prevent that from happening is to keep the people happy with an occasional show of good will.

Don't get me wrong. I'm not trying to sell you on the idea that I'm one of those loyal Jewish patriots. I couldn't care less about the freedom of the people, as long as I'm enjoying my own freedom. I landed in prison for crimes committed in my own interest. Never mind exactly what my crimes were! That's none of your business. You can figure it out for yourself that I wasn't sentenced to death for petty larceny!

What I'm saying is that I don't feel I owe Pilate any debt of gratitude for my release. His "Passover amnesty" is just a gimmick, purely in his own interest. Besides, Pilate didn't really want me released. Things just didn't work out the way he had them figured. When he gave the people a choice between me and Jesus, he didn't think I had the chance of a snowball in hell.

You see, Pilate wanted Jesus released, because Jesus was obviously innocent of the charges against Him. Pilate thought he had found an easy solution to his dilemma by giving the people a choice between me and Jesus. But the people were so insistent on Jesus' crucifixion that Pilate was afraid to go against their wishes. You should have seen the look on his face when the crowd hollered, "Release Barabbas! Crucify Jesus!" He was flabbergasted. But he had given his word to let the people have their choice, and there was no way he could safely renege on his promise.

So here I am, free as a bird, "The People's Choice." Now maybe you think I should go around thanking the people, or the priests who stirred them up to make the choice they did? Well, I may have thought so at first, but not for long. For a while I thought some of my old buddies had been supporting me, doing a snow job on the people, selling them on the idea that I'm a pretty nice guy after all, maybe even innocent of the murders for which I was convicted.

I should have known better. My former fairweather friends hightailed it out of here the day I was arrested, and haven't been seen since. And I found out quick enough that it wasn't my popularity that got me my freedom. As I said before, nobody even wants to talk to me. It's almost as though their conscience starts bothering them every time they see me standing here, while Jesus is hanging there. No, these people aren't any friends of mine. They wouldn't accept my thanks, even if I wanted to give it—which I don't.

For some reason, the crowd hated the Nazarene enough to turn me loose in order to get Him crucified. I think if I had been the devil himself, the mob would have picked me over Jesus, considering the mood they were in. No, I don't owe my freedom to Pilate's generosity, nor to the people's love. If anything, I owe it to their hate, their savage, bitter hate for that man on the cross.

Now this has really got my curiosity aroused, and that's why I'm still here, trying to figure out what He did to deserve such hatred. To begin with, He was obviously innocent of the charge that was raised against Him in Pilate's court. Pilate is no dummy. He knew that if someone really posed a threat to the Romans, these people would aid and abet such a man, rather than turn him in. That's why Pilate delcared Jesus innocent after a brief examination. And King Herod, who had a chance to examine Jesus, evidently agreed with Piate's verdict of innocence.

The Nazarene's crime, if He committed one, was not political. And it wasn't a personal crime against people either. From what I've been able to find out, He never killed or robbed anyone. Just the opposite. He is said to have healed many.

The most amazing thing I've noticed about Jesus is the way He is taking it all. Not once did He scream when He was being scourged, and believe me, a Roman scourging is enough to make the most hardened criminal scream his head off, begging for mercy. Jesus didn't even curse the crowd or Pilate for the unfairness of His trial. And I've been watching Him up there on the cross. Once He cried out asking God to forgive these people who are crucifying Him. Do you see that weeping woman beneath the cross? That's His mother. Jesus was concerned about who would take care of her now. Can you imagine worrying about anyone else while you're hanging there, suffering all the agony of hell on that cross? Look at that thief on the cross next to Jesus—the one on the right. Jesus said something to him—I couldn't make out what He said—but it obviously gave the thief a feeling of great relief and peace. It's almost as if he lost his fear of death on account of whatever it was that the Nazarene said to him.

You want my opinion? I'm convinced that the reason for Jesus being there on the cross is a religious one, and that it has something to do with His being called Jesus the Christ. For centuries our people have been waiting for someone to come who would be the Savior of the nation. The prophets who wrote our sacred Scriptures told of a Messiah or Christ who would come.

It seems that Jesus claimed to be that Messiah. In fact, I have it on good authority that the high priest found Jesus deserving of death for blasphemy because He called Himself the Son of God. The charge was changed to treason and sedition when they brought Jesus into Pilate's court, because Pilate, being a Roman and uninterested in Jewish religious matters, wouldn't have paid any attention to a charge of blasphemy and would immediately have thrown the case out of court.

Those Sadducee priests on the Sanhedrin are a power-hungry bunch and don't really care that much about whether the Messiah ever comes or not. They probably regarded Jesus as a threat to their own positions of authority. And the Pharisees on the Sanhedrin probably resented the fact that Jesus did not go along with all of their traditions that they hold so sacred. And a lot of the common people were probably disappointed when Jesus didn't succeed in raising an army to drive out the Romans.

Still, there must also have been a lot of mob hysteria in their bloodthirsty insistence on Jesus' crucifixion. Some of them had hailed Jesus with Hosannas as the Son of David, as the Messiah, only a few days before they were screaming for His blood.

On the way here some women openly displayed their sympathy with Jesus. And even now some of these people are beginning to act as though they feel they made a mistake in condemning Him. I think that's why they try to avoid me. I'm a walking reminder to them that they may be guilty of crucifying their own Messiah.

That still leaves unanswered the big question: "Who is this Jesus of Nazareth, anyway?" If it weren't for Him, I wouldn't be standing here, that's for sure. As long as I live, I'll never get Him off my mind. What if He *was* the Messiah? Or what if He still *is* the Messiah? This may not be the end of the Nazarene. He said He would rise from the grave. Some of the priests have been ridiculing Him about that. But I know they are already making arrangements to have a guard posted at the entrance to His tomb. So they must halfway believe it themselves. I think I'll just hang around for a few more days before I leave town.

Note: We don't know whether or not Barabbas watched the crucifixion of Jesus. It seems reasonable that normal curiosity might have driven him to follow the crowd to Calvary. And we don't know what conclusions he may have reached in his contemplation of Jesus. It certainly is possible that Jesus, who saved Barabbas from crucifixion, may also have saved him from eternal death. We know what happened in the case of that other criminal—one of the two crucified with Jesus. We have Jesus' word for that, because we know what our Savior said to the thief that put peace in his heart. Even better than that, we know what He says to us through His inspired apostle: "Believe on the Lord Jesus Christ, and thou shalt be saved!"

PETER

The time: About A.D. 68
The place: A prison in Rome

Welcome in Jesus' name! I'm glad you've come. Yes, I'm Simon Peter. It's a good thing you found me today. Tomorrow would have been too late, for I am to be executed—crucified. Oh, please don't be sorry for me! I'm quite ready to die. So many of our original band of 12 apostles have led the way.

James was the first to go—beheaded by order of King Herod. My brother Andrew was crucified six years ago in Greece. Of the others I've heard rumors. Philip is said to have been hanged. Simon Zelotes was cut in half. Bartholomew was skinned alive. All of them died rejoicing to be counted worthy of martyrdom.

No, don't be sorry for me. I'm honored that Andrew and I, who followed Jesus for so many years, follow Him now also in the manner of death—on the cross. My faithful wife, always at my side, died several years ago, and I look forward to a reunion in heaven. I agree with Paul, "For me to die is gain." At my age and under these circumstances death is a release and a reward.

I'm very thankful for having been granted these 40 years to tell the world that Jesus, who was crucified, lives and that we have eternal life through faith in Him. I'm thankful too for my friend Paul, whom the Lord used so mightily in bringing the Gospel to the Gentiles. He was beheaded only a few months ago by order of Emperor Nero. What a blessing to the world that he wrote so many beautiful letters, full of the teaching of Jesus! I myself wrote two letters, which I hope you will read. I am not as scholarly as Paul, but Jesus has used me, as He will use you too, if you love Him and let Him be the master of your life.

I have told my young friend and traveling companion, John Mark, all that Jesus did of which I was an eyewitness, and he has undertaken to write it all down for posterity—as Matthew, likewise an eyewitness and an apostle, has done. Likewise John, my dear partner and friend, still alive and well, thank God, will I am sure write what needs to be written in order that many may believe that Jesus is the Christ, the Son of God, and, believing, have life through His name.

My friends, treasure these gospels and epistles as you treasure the writings of the prophets, and study them diligently, for all these Scriptures are by inspiration of God. They are words of truth and life.

I know you want me to tell you about my association with Jesus. I'm always glad to do that, but where shall I begin? Our time here is limited, so let me focus on that last night together before Jesus was crucified.

Jesus wanted to eat the Passover meal with the 12 of us, so John and I went into town, following His instructions to the letter, and made the necessary preparations. You know, of course, that our Passover was a very symbolic festival in more ways than one. As a feast of remembrance it reminded us of that night in Egypt when our people were spared by the Angel of Death, who killed the firstborn in every Egyptian home but passed over the homes of our people which were marked by the blood of a lamb.

But the festival was also prophetic, in that the blood of the Passover lamb, which saved our people from death then, was symbolic of the blood of the Lamb of God, the Messiah, whose blood would save us from eternal death.

At the time I don't think we fully realized that this was the most significant Passover ever celebrated. We were eating the Passover lamb in the presence of the real Lamb of God. That night prophecy and fulfillment were joined.

How dense we all were!—I above all. John the Baptist, whose disciples we had been before we began to follow Jesus, had directed us to the Lord with the words: "Behold the Lamb of God, who takes away the sins of the world!" And Jesus Himself had more than once told us quite plainly that He would be killed in Jerusalem in fulfillment of the prophecies concerning the Messiah. But somehow it didn't quite penetrate our minds.

I guess we just couldn't bear the thought that Jesus must die. I know I couldn't. Once, when He said He was going to be killed, I burst out with more love in my heart than understanding in my mind: "Lord, this will never happen to You!" And Jesus slapped me down with words as harsh as any He ever used in dealing with His worst enemies: "Get away, Satan! For yours are not the thoughts of God!" I was in a state of shock until I understood that His rebuke was an act of love. By saying that He should not be killed, I was in effect denying Him as the Messiah of Scripture. I needed to be straightened out.

After this Passover the festival lost much of its prophetic meaning. Now that the prophecies of the Messiah are fulfilled in Jesus, we have the Messiah Himself and have no further need for the symbol. And so Jesus started a new thing for us to observe and celebrate—a supper in commemoration of His death for our sins.

He took the bread and the wine that were on the table, gave us each to eat and drink, and said: "This is My body and blood, given and shed for the forgiveness of your sins." He told us to continue the celebration of this meaningful sacramental meal, and we did. And I hope that you still do, for the very necessary strengthening of your faith and as a frequent reminder of the sacrifice Jesus made for you on the cross.

We 12 disciples often had our arguments and differences of opinion, but we were all saddened when Jesus announced that one of us was betraying Him. Who would have thought it possible? And we were really shaken when Jesus said that all of us would be offended that night and forsake Him.

I was never one to be at a loss for words, although I often managed to put my foot in my mouth. That's what I did here, when I said that even if the others would be offended, I never would be; and that I would die before I'd forsake Him. Jesus just looked at me sadly and said ever so gently: "Before the cock crows twice tonight, Peter, you will three times deny that you know Me." Well, that seemed so preposterous at the time that I quickly put it out of my mind.

After we had left the Upper Room and walked to a point outside the city on the slope of the Mount of Olives, Jesus took James and John and me into the garden called Gethsemane. The others waited near the entrance. Now Jesus became very sad and depressed, and went off by Himself to kneel and pray to the Father. We would have tried to comfort Him, if we had known what to say; but what could we do? At that time we were not even able to fathom the depth of His anguish.

Finally the moment came that Jesus had been prophesying, and a band of men sent out by the high priest, and led by Judas, of all people, came to arrest Jesus. This seemed like a moment that called for physical action; and so with more strength of arm than of brain or spirit, I pulled out my sword and began hacking away at one of Jesus' adversaries. I'd show Jesus that I would not forsake Him and that I was ready to die, if need be, in His defense!

But what followed took all the heart out of me. Instead of encouraging me to fight on, Jesus told me to put up my sword, and He healed the wound I had inflicted on Malchus, the high priest's servant. Jesus said that if He needed help, His Father would provide it. Overwhelmed by hurt pride and frustration, I ran away, as did the rest of our group.

Even as I ran, with the cool wind whipping my face and clearing the cobwebs from my befuddled brain, I recognized the simple truth of Jesus' words: He didn't need me. It was I who needed Him.

And so it came that I went to the palace of Caiaphas and Annas, where Jesus was taken. John, who knew his way around, got me admitted into the courtyard, where I warmed myself at a fire, waiting to see what would happen next.

What followed is difficult for me to talk about, even now. I'll make it short. When some of the servants began to question me and to charge me with being one of Jesus' disciples, I panicked and with cursing and swearing denied that I knew Jesus or understood what they were talking about. Just as a rooster, awakening to the dawn, crowed for the second time, Jesus was led through the courtyard on the way from the court of Annas to that of Caiaphas. He just looked at me. . . .

Half-blinded by hot tears of shame, I stumbled out into the cold early morning light and wept as though my heart would break. It was the most dreadful moment of my entire life. No sickness, no pain, no bereavement—nothing could compare with that anguish. All that kept me from despair and suicide was the remembrance of the Sacrament that Jesus had instituted only hours before, and which was, as He said, for the forgiveness of sins—for the forgiveness even of my awful sin!

You know the rest. They crucified my Lord. But death could not hold Him, and He rose from the grave, as He said He would, and He lives. Of that I am an eyewitness, as are my fellow apostles and many others. You know what has happened to many of them, and I've told you what's going to happen to me tomorrow. Perhaps my story will help you to understand why no sacrifice could be too great, no hardship too difficult to endure, when it comes to witnessing to the fact that Christ Jesus is both Lord and Savior of all who trust in Him.

They'll be coming for me soon. You'd better go now. God bless and keep you. I'll see you again one day. Farewell!

SAINT JOHN

Costumes are not essential, yet they lend an atmosphere that aids the congregation in accepting the characterization as a portrayal of a person from another time and place.

If done in street clothes, perhaps John could wear a clerical collar and even liturgical vestments, since this portrayal is intended for a Communion celebration during Lent. If a costume is preferred, John should wear a long tunic with a girdle, a brightly colored sash at the waist. No sandals.

In this portrayal several ushers will be needed to bring in the picnic table that is placed in the lower chancel. Benches are grouped around it. A redwood patio table will work very nicely, but if that is not available, use the regular kind of folding table used by most churches. A table cloth, dishes, silverware, etc., will be set while the monolog continues. The acolyte or another young lad should be close at hand for the foot washing event. A pitcher and basin are needed for this. Improvise from supplies in the kitchen.

As the monolog opens, John follows the ushers carrying the table into the lower chancel, giving careful directions along the way. The houselights are dimmed, and a spotlight is focused on John.

The text for this service might be John 14:25-31 or John 15:12-17.

SAINT JOHN

Yes, that's it! Bring the table right here, and the benches too. Now let me see, I think we can put the cloth on the table; and you there, get the dishes and set the table for 13. There were (counting on his fingers) 12 of us disciples, and Jesus, of course, so set it as it was that night.

(John looks up, as if noticing the assembled congregation for the first time.)

Ah, you're already here (said as if surprised). I had hoped to have everything ready before you came, but I'm afraid I'm a little tardy.

You see, the altar there (pointing to it) is set for your celebration of Holy Communion tonight. It's set the way you customarily celebrate the Sacrament, and that's fine. I only wanted to add another dimension to your experience of Maundy Thursday this evening. I wanted you to have a glimpse into the Upper Room, and to use your imagination to recall with me the marvel of that night when Jesus transformed the Passover Seder into a Sacrament of forgiveness.

(John is seated on one of the benches.)

The tableware is modern, as you can see. Yet it is a fact that it was a meal, yes, a banquet to which we sat down, a holy recalling of that night centuries before when the Angel of the Lord passed over the homes of the faithful Israelites in Egypt and invaded the homes of the unfaithful with death. Our meal was a symbolic dinner party.

The setting is still not quite right. It was essential that we reclined while dining, to remind us of the rest God gave us after our exodus from the land of slavery. Each couch was pushed up to the center table from which we helped ourselves to the variety of dishes offered. At other times we sat on crude benches. There were times when in place of couches we had pillows on which to lie and the table was centrally placed and rather low. The method depended on the traditions of the household, as well as what could be afforded. Our borrowed banquet hall was not fancy, but it was somewhat nicer than the plainest home.

We did not use individualized eating utensils. (Picking up a fork and staring at it.) Our fingers worked very nicely, and we frequently used a common bowl from which we dipped with our fingers to obtain a mouthful of nourishment. You fastidious people probably cringe at such an idea, but it really was a very cordial way in which to dine. You never had to worry that someone had kept the choice servings for himself.

(Rises and moves to another position.) However, the reason I am here is not to dwell on the details of the setting. It is what happened in that Upper Room that you remember and are interested in.

You won't find more information about the Passover meal itself in my Gospel. Matthew, Mark, and Luke have already written about it, as well as Paul. I filled in the message our Lord spoke to us, as well as His high-priestly prayer, where (among many things) He prayed for unity among the faithful. I reported the foot washing. Here (calling to one of those who helped bring in the table), bring me the basin and the pitcher. Be seated.

(John rises, takes a cloth, and girds himself with it. He kneels before his friend, who is barefoot. Placing the basin under one foot, he pours water over it and dries it gently with a towel. He repeats it for the second foot while speaking.)

It was a simple act of hospitality. One never invited guests to his house and then ignored the courtesy of foot washing. It just wasn't done. However, Simon the Pharisee up in Galilee neglected to do that for the Master. Jesus accepted the oversight in a kindly fashion, yet other Jews would have thought it a gross insult. Now, on this Thursday night, Jesus Himself took the role of foot washer.

I'm afraid the rest of us thought we were too important for so demeaning a task. Not Jesus. (Chuckling to himself.) He rolled up His sleeves, got down on His knees, and went from disciple to disciple to cleanse them of the grime collected on the dusty roads and dirty streets of Jerusalem. "I have given you an example," He said, "that you also should do as I have done to you. Truly, truly, I say to you, a servant is not greater than his master; nor is he who is sent greater than he who sent him."

It was a humbling experience. He was frequently reminding us that humility is the virtue that denotes His followers, for no one can truly love others who is unwilling to serve them actively.

(John picks up a loaf of bread and breaks it. This should be an unleavened loaf baked for this occasion.)

To break bread at a meal and to share salt were well-understood symbols. They meant more than what they mean to most people today. It was our Oriental way of claiming fellowship. To eat bread and share salt with others was to declare our forgiveness of past injuries. It was an expression of reconciliation.

To break bread at the Passover intensified that understanding, yet it had a broader meaning, for it identified all the celebrants as members of the chosen people. For centuries our people had observed Passover. It was a holy occasion to teach each generation about our uniqueness as the people of God. We celebrated it within the home rather than at the synagog. It was a family event, and so for the benefit of the children a variety of symbolic foods was assembled to relive the historic past. They were object lessons that reminded us of solemn events and a sacred destiny.

A paschal lamb was slain, and the temple priests caught the blood and poured it out at the altar. The lamb was then brought home for the feast. No bones were broken. No less than 10 and no more than 20 guests were to gather for the Passover, for actually one lamb could not feed more than that, and all had to be consumed. Bitter herbs were eaten, such as chicory, lettuce, or endive, to remind us of the bitter bondage our people experienced as Egyptian slaves. Unleavened loaves dipped in a sweet sauce reminded us of the Promised Land. The *haroset,* a paste of apples and nuts, reminded us of the mortar used by the Jews in laboring for Pharaoh.

The room was comfortably fixed for us. The sweet aroma of the *haroset* and the roasted lamb filled the hall. It was an awesome moment, and I shall not soon forget the mood of that meal or the way in which our Lord's final days among us unfolded. When He finished washing our feet, He began to tell us some disquieting news: "I say to you, one of you will betray Me!" His face was deeply troubled, and His eyes testified to inner turmoil and aching hurt. We all glanced at one another. I was reclining close to the Lord, and Peter asked me to tell who it was that Jesus was speaking about, so I inquired, "Lord, who is it?"

I was transfixed by His answer: "It is he to whom I shall give this morsel when I have dipped it." Simon Iscariot's son, Judas, received the helping.

"What you are going to do, do quickly," said the Lord.

It was puzzling to us. Why did Jesus say that? Some thought He had sent Judas on an errand to buy something for the feast, or to give alms to the poor. We were unprepared for the betrayal that came, even though the Master forewarned us. It is difficult to believe you are a witness to so horrendous an event.

During the Passover meal three cups of the best wine (but watered down) were to be drunk. The first cup was blessed by the father and passed around the table. The second cup was drunk after the Hallel was sung, two ancient psalms, followed by a prayer of thanksgiving. The third cup was blessed, and during the drinking of the fourth cup Psalms 115—118 were sung. A younger person would ask an older one, "Why is this night different from all other nights?" To that he responded, "We were slaves . . . in Egypt, and the Eternal, our God, led us from there with a mighty hand."

It was the Passover meal, but Jesus transformed it from merely a historic recollection of an event long past to a relevant experience of forgiveness for right now. He took the bread and blessed it. "Take, eat; this is My body," He said. Lifting the chalice and repeating His blessing, He shared it with all of us, saying: "This cup is the new covenant in My blood."

The words were startling to us. It was not the past recalled. It was a future envisioned. It was as though the Angel of Death were passing over us anew, for we were marked as were the doorposts of those houses with the blood of sacrifice. It was hard for us to understand that our Paschal Lamb would be Jesus, yet after Pentecost we well understood what our Lord was saying to us. He was to be the Sacrifice that atoned for the sins of all. You see why I say the setting was not as important as the event? Still I want you to experience some of the aura of that night.

"Let not your hearts be troubled," said Jesus in beginning His message to us. "Believe in God, believe also in Me. In My Father's house are many rooms; if it were not so, would I have told you that I go to prepare a place for you?" He promised to come again to take us to Himself. Then our marvelous Lord made a statement that most of us could not quite accept. "And you know the way where I am going," He said. Thomas spoke up, "Lord, we do not know where You are going; how can we know the way?"

The response was unforgettable. "I am the way, and the truth, and the life," He answered; "no one comes to the Father but by Me."

Throughout this conversational message, Jesus dialoged with us, assuring us of His ongoing presence and our ability to minister effectively. "Whatever you ask in My name, I will do it, that the Father may be glorified in the Son," He said assertively. "I will not leave you desolate," He said. "The Counselor, the Holy Spirit, whom the Father will send in My name, He will teach you all things and bring to your remembrance all that I have said to you." "Let not your hearts be troubled, neither let them be afraid."

He told us to expect difficulty. He confided to us that being His emissaries would not be easy. Persecution and hatred would dog our steps. "When the Spirit of truth comes, He will guide you into all the truth," Jesus assured us. "He will glorify Me, for He will take what is Mine and declare it to you. All that the Father has is Mine; therefore I said that He will take what is Mine and declare it to you."

We were hearing the well-laid plans of God, and it was too much for us to grasp at the time. Our Teacher was to be taken from us, and all we could consider was how and why. It was as night turned into day when we later began to understand the full impact of those momentous words.

(Rises and goes to the pulpit.)

It was an evening of quiet remembrance, but it became more than that. It was for us that sacred encounter of man with God that none who makes it can forget.In that hour Jesus reached His fullest stature. He was more than what we had dared accept before, and fully what we had hoped Him to be. He was and is the redemptive Messiah. The feast that night was for you as well as the Twelve. That banquet was a farewell dinner party that becomes for each of us a welcoming celebration. In the Sacrament, Jesus frees us from sin and guilt so we can make our exodus into His Promised Land of spiritual joy.

Tonight, my friends, you are in that Upper Room where the Lord took the meal, the Old Covenant, and transformed it into the sacramental meal, the New Covenant. You are there, and you are as close by His side as I was, for you are His chosen ones and He gives you a place of honor. You are there, for Jesus is present. You can recapture some of the elements of that momentous evening in the love that fills this room, the excitement, the expectancy of a sacred encounter, one in which He provides blessing upon blessing, joy in the midst of personal pain, forgiveness in the reality of sin.

From the cross comes a light that illuminates this Sacrament as the sublimest experience of spiritual growth. Jesus is here! Let's celebrate! The Passover has come; let us rejoice and realize that beyond the dignity of our worship is that bright new commandment that gives us the hope and freedom to inspire our jubilation. Said Jesus that night and this night: "A new commandment I give to you, that you love one another; even as I have loved you, that you also love one another. By this all men will know that you are My disciples, if you have love for one another."

Love your neighbors—greet them with a word of Christian love, and experience for yourself the love that goes beyond all expectation, that absolves the repentant sinner, that confers upon him sonship and peace!

Yes, that is what this night means to me. It is more than a table set for feasting, more than a banquet hall decorated with festoons of celebration. It means Jesus the Christ redeems me, and loves me beyond anything I can imagine.

Let it be that kind of night for you also.

Come, take that table away. For we are not going to focus upon the past any longer. It is the present. Your need is now. Jesus made preparation long ago so that each subsequent celebration of His Supper would not be merely a time to look back, but a time to look ahead. In forgiveness you can look forward to renewed vigor. Time wasted in guilty revery may now be spent in actions of thanksgiving, in deeds of love, in inspired activity in His behalf. You have a new tomorrow each time you sup at His table. He picked up the tab. He paid the price. It was not, as you often do, put on a credit card. The sacrifice was made, paid in full.

Come, then, and know that the Angel of Death has passed over. In Christ we are freed from slavery to sin and are guided to the Promised Land of God's grace, the fellowship of the redeemed. The Paschal Lamb has been sacrificed. The unleavened bread is ready. The wine has been poured. The table is set. Come. Jesus invites you. He said: "These things I have spoken to you that My joy may be in you and that your joy may be full." Amen.

LAZARUS

The setting for Lazarus is the most unusual of the series. Drape an 8-foot banquet table with a large white sheet. Place it in the lower chancel. If possible, for this service keep the houselights dimmed except for the chancel until after the portrayal.

Lazarus, wearing a white robe (instead of the strips of cloth binding the Jewish corpse) lies on the table, which simulates a tomb. He is absolutely still, totally immobile until his part is to be played. Then with excitement and joy he slowly arises and exclaims, "I'm alive!"

The atmosphere of the church will become absolutely electric. From beginning to end, every eye and ear will be intent on the message. Death is real, but so is the power of the Savior. People want to know that and are eager to hear it over and over again.

Some pastors possess the long while linen chasuble that is used in hot weather in lieu of all the other Eucharistic vestments underneath. This makes an excellent shroud. It can also be made from a sheet. Simply make a place for head and arms. Wear white tee shirt and white jeans underneath.

I would not suggest using street clothes to portray this character. Too much of the impact would be lost. Since his costuming can be done so simply with materials everyone has available, Lazarus need not be "contemporized."

Lazarus leaves the "tomb" and talks to the people from the lower chancel. If notes are needed, he may stand in back of the "tomb," which serves as a good place to locate white paper that will not be distracting to the congregation. Other directions are also given in the script.

Play Lazarus as enthusiastic, full of life, grateful for his special revelation of the Lord's majestic power over life and death.

The text for this service might be John 11:39-44.

LAZARUS

(As the monolog begins, Lazarus, who has been stretched out on the bier throughout the opening of the service, slowly arises. He speaks as though awed at first, as if Jesus has just commanded him to come forth, then with rising crescendo.)

I'm alive!

I'm really alive! I'm alive again!

Oh, my friends, I can't tell you what all has happened to me these last days and what exhilaration I feel, what total exhilaration!

I'm alive! Can you believe that? (Walking down to the front of the congregation; offering himself . . .) Pinch my flesh and see for yourself that I am no spirit returned from the dead, no apparition of the mind, no false hope or vision of the soul. I'm alive, fully, tremendously! Though it happened long ago, I still marvel at the miracle. I was bound in strips of cloth, a kind of shroud. I wear this robe as a constant reminder of my resurrection. But now the dead live! I *was* dead, asleep in faith, but literally dead. The miracle is that never before has a man been in his tomb for four days and arisen!

(He returns to the "bier" and speaks from the other side, facing the congregation.)

Believe me, I was clinically dead. My vital signs were nil. I was neither comatose nor unconscious. I had died, and I still remember the agony, the suffering that I went through. The illness I had was a debilitating one. When it struck, it sapped me immediately of my strength, so that I could not stir from my bed. My sisters, Mary and Martha, lavished their care on me.

They provided cold compresses for my aching, feverish head; sips of cooling water from the well; visits from physicians from Jerusalem, but a scant two miles from our home in Bethany. All of these were loving actions provided by caring sisters, who thought enough of me to even send a messenger to Jesus (who was across the Jordan) to come and aid me.

But before He came, I died. I can't tell you what it was like. It was as ethereal as one can imagine, a vague kind of advancing down a long, mystical tunnel, and yet I was neither sad nor feeling the distress of my illness any longer. It seemed so peaceful, so beautiful, so vastly different from life that I could not regret my last breath. I was asleep, but in a sense that was profoundly restful. I died, but there was no regretting it. I slipped away into something that becomes so inexplicable that I can only remember the absence of regret.

How often I had heard the Lord speak of the kingdom of heaven! Frequently, when He visited Jerusalem, He was a guest in our home. Bethany is a suburb of the great city. My sisters were fascinated by His message, and I was intrigued by His mastery of life, His insights into eternity and the things of the Eternal Father. Never before had I met a rabbi like Him! We were well aware He was no ordinary rabbi, and the more we heard the more we were convinced He was the Promised One, the Messiah of God.

My sisters knew that Jesus, besides being my close friend, would offer me spiritual comfort in my dying moments. They sent for Him, and they were indeed distressed when He didn't come right away.

We were told by His followers that He knew how gravely ill I was, and had even told them, "Our friend Lazarus has fallen asleep," and then had said a curious thing: ". . . but I go to awake him out of sleep." The disciples did not realize He was referring to my death; they thought He meant ordinary sleep. "Lord, if he has fallen asleep, he will recover," they said.

Jesus, always a comfort to the ignorant, always a counselor to the unknowing, explained that my "sleep"' was no ordinary sleep.

"Lazarus is dead; and for your sake I am glad that I was not there, so that you may believe." They must have thought those words to be cruel indeed, for they could not understand the full meaning of what He said. "Let us go to him," He said finally. It was Thomas who then encouraged the frightened disciples to go along, for they knew that within Jerusalem's walls were people of responsibility, religious leaders, conniving for His death.

When they arrived in Bethany, they learned that I had been entombed four long, sorrowful days. Martha scolded Jesus for His delay. "Lord, if You had been here, my brother would not have died," she said. The pain of the loss was deeply etched in her rueful words. Yet Martha's faith, though tried, had not disappeared. "Even now I know that whatever You ask from God, God will give You," said that sister of mine.

Jesus touched her hand to comfort her, for she was deeply troubled. "Your brother will rise again," He told her.

Martha believed that fully. "I know that he will rise again in the resurrection at the last day," she responded.

And then the marvel of that truth was sharpened to the point of a spear. "I am the resurrection and the life," said Jesus; "he who believes in Me, though he die, yet shall he live, and whoever lives and believes in Me shall never die." "Do you believe this?" He asked her.

"Yes, Lord," she sighed, "I believe that You are the Christ, the Son of God, He who is coming into the world."

Jesus asked for Mary, and together with an entourage of mourners she came weeping. Her greeting was an echo of Martha's: "Lord, if You had been here, my brother would not have died." John tells me that he saw how troubled and deeply moved in spirit the Lord was with those words, and seeing the sorrow of my family and friends, He wept also. They showed Him my tomb, cut deep into a mountain like a tunnel that descends downward at an angle into two rock-hewn rooms.

Some of the mourners murmured, "Could not He who opened the eyes of the blind man have kept this man from dying?"

I probably would have asked the same thing. He had healed so many of their plaguing ills. He had called others to life, but they had only been dead a short while. My friends despaired, for I had been dead four days, and in their weakness they faltered. But this is what Jesus came to prove—that He is truly Lord over all and that despite the decay, despite the decomposition, He has mastery to rule over life and death. He asked that the stone be removed, and then reminded my sisters: "Did I not tell you that if you would believe you would see the glory of God?"

Then He prayed with earnestness, thankful that the Father had heard His request, so that those standing about might believe.

(Lazarus moves to the front of the chancel, standing before the "bier.")

It was then in the still yet serene splendor of death that I heard with my dead ears. It was then that I felt the revival of life within me, calling me back out of that long ethereal tunnel. The blood rushed in my body; the quieted heart stirred to action; my pulse began to throb within my arms and legs. The vagueness of my mind was dispelled. I had heard my name. I was called to do something, to get up, to move (excitedly), and burst the lock of death. My Christ was calling to me, and my unsteady limbs strengthened as I strained against the bands of cloth, for the stone chambers echoed and reverberated with Christ's mighty invitation: "Lazarus, come out."

My hands and feet were bound with bandages, and my face was wrapped with a cloth. At the Lord's instruction many hands rushed to unbind me and set me free to live again.

My sisters hugged me, and tears of joy flowed effusively. My friends were awe-struck. (He moves closer to the congregation.) I shall never forget the look on the faces of my neighbors. Their eyes fairly popped out of their heads. Some knelt, but most were too stunned to say or do anything. They didn't know whether to touch me or not, for to touch a dead body makes a Jew ceremonially unclean. I assured them I was alive again. It was a moment of exhilaration, of great joy, of sublime wonder. I gave my life and soul anew to Jesus; I offered Him my wealth and all I had, but He wanted none of these things, except my faith, my love, my thanksgiving. These He had.

Permit me to tell you, you who sorrow, that Jesus wipes away the tears, comforting the believer, enabling us to see beyond the vague mist of death to His conquest in our behalf.

Sorrow and tears always accompany death, yet Christians need not fear it; for though separation is an aching hurt, reunion with the Lord is too marvelous to drown with unending sorrow. We mourn and rejoice simultaneously.

Jesus went on from Bethany to Jerusalem, to Calvary, to the tomb, and the miracle of resurrection was repeated all over again, but this time it was the fulfillment of Messianic prophecy, as He willingly offered Himself for crucifixion, the Lamb of God atoning for the sins of the world. He rose from the dead and thereby conquered death. He is the Lord of life.

(With emphasis) I am alive, but the life the Savior promises us beyond death is not an end, for it is a triumphal arch, an open gate, an unlocked door, a new birth, an entry into a life that will never know death again. It is the gift the Lord has won for all mankind, but only the faithful possess the key, for it is by believing in the Conqueror of death that the door to eternal bliss opens to us.

(Parades in front of the congregation.) You have undoubtedly seen few men return from the grave. I was returned to life to live out my days in Bethany, to enjoy the continuing fellowship of my neighbors and sisters, and to manage my lands and flocks and vineyards. Jesus returned to life to give birth to an endless fellowship with the faithful, and to manage the lives of those who trust Him. (He returns to lectern.)

I am Lazarus of Bethany on the Mount of Olives. In Hebrew my name is Eleazar, which means "God has helped." God has helped me to know that death need never be feared, that faith is the conquering weapon, that Jesus is not only my Savior, my Redeemer, the One who has given me new life, but He is the One who calls all of us to eternity to live with Him forever. He it is who loves us so much that death cannot stop His caring, but provides an abundant and eternal rest with Him in heaven.

You with the long faces, celebrate life! It's to be lived, not regretted; enjoyed, not despaired. (He speaks with enthusiasm.)

You who dread each day because of the drudgery you see as your lot, live a little! Live triumphantly in Christ. Live victoriously in faith. Know the challenge of each day, the hope He offers, the encouragement He gives. LIVE!

(Growing serious) If He could call me from the dead, if He could command me to life again after rotting four days in the pit of the earth, can He not resurrect you from your anguish, your inner turmoils, your depression and bland existence? Of course He can!

Listen to Him! Today He is calling you to the celebration of forever! He wants to revive your hope and to conquer your fear of death by letting you know through me that the conquest is real.

My resurrection was reported to the Pharisees, and the chief priests were indignant. They were wrong to be afraid of Jesus, for He loved them dearly; but they would have none of it, and so they plotted His death, the bitter death of crucifixion, which was indeed far more hideous than my death from disease. Jesus went on then to Ephraim with His disciples, and in the days that followed He made His triumphant entry into the Holy City, and by week's end He was nailed to a cross only to arise with the fulness of life by Easter. They could nail Him to a cross, but they could not keep the lid sealed on His tomb.

My friends, here is the message I wish to leave with you. I live. I am alive. But it was only the Lord Jesus and His love for me that made it happen. Let the power of His resurrection give life to your body. Arise from your tombs of gloom; Christ commands it. My dearest friends, don't mourn for the dead in Christ. Rejoice for them, for they have been given life forever.

That's love.

It was love that called me to life.

It is love that calls you to live fully too, the life in Christ.

(Lazarus returns to the other side of the "bier" and prays.)

When you summoned me from the bowels of the earth, from my sleep in death, O Lord, you quickened my lifeless form. My lungs filled with air. My stomach growled. My parched mouth ached for a sip. My heart raced, and the blood flowed, and life rushed through me.

Thank You, Jesus, for using me to show to all the world the power at Your command. Thank You for giving us that certain hope that becomes reality as our death is swallowed up in Your victory.

Aid my faith by Your Spirit so that it may withstand the temptation to always reason logically, for there is no logic in a love so strong that it dies to assure eternal life to repentant sinners. Give me the power to rely on it even if I don't understand it. Call me forth from tombs of gloomy depression and disbelief to be alive in Christ all over again. Say to me and to all those like me: Beloved, come out! Amen.

SIMON THE CYRENE

A simple tunic with a brightly striped cloak, fastened at the waist with a cincture or sash, would be appropriate for Simon. Fashion a turban about the head as a distinctive North African feature. Simon wears sandals.

If street dress is preferred, you may garb him in a blue collar outfit. He comes from North Africa, and although he is not a poor man, he is not afraid to soil his hands.

Simon varies his position from time to time. The setting is simple and requires only a Lenten cross in large size or miniature. You may wish to give the worshipers a small remembrance of the service. Little wooden crosses made by one of your carpenters would be inexpensive and a nice memento. You would have to plan this early in the season, however.

Simon is an assertive person. No meek mouse either in physical capability or verbalization. Play him strong-willed and positive.

The text for the service might be Matthew 27:32-36.

SIMON THE CYRENE

Yes, yes, that's very much like the cross on which Jesus the Nazarene hung. (Simon stares at the Lenten cross, or a small rough-hewn hand-held cross.) The Romans had more than one style of cross, you know. (He continues to stand by it.)

It was an instrument of execution throughout the Mediterranean world. The Assyrians, Egyptians, Greeks, and even the Phoenicians of Carthage used it. Sometimes it was merely a stake with no crossbar at all. Sometimes it was a crosspiece that was placed on top of a stake that remained permanently in place. At other times it was like the one you see here—a cross of two unequal pieces. It was on the top piece that the superscription was nailed, "The King of the Jews."

You see, the stake was imbedded into the hard, rocky ground. It was difficult to put up and just as difficult to dislodge. It was always outside the city walls and near a highway to make it easier for the executioners to get their job done. Frequently the doomed prisoner was forced to carry the crosspiece to the site of crucifixion himself, a double indignity, and then it was attached to the stake. (Gesturing) The Romans called the upright the *staticulum*, and the arms were termed the *patibulum*. It was this loathsome load they made Jesus carry along the Way of Sorrows to Golgotha.

It was that burdensome piece they also forced *me* to carry. (He goes to lectern.)

I was visiting the city of Jerusalem for Passover. You see, I'm from North Africa, from Cyrene, a city on the coast of what you today call Libya. We had quite a large Jewish population there, mostly merchants and some vintners. I had journeyed to Jerusalem to fulfill tradition and celebrate the Passover. I had been there before, but it seemed particularly important that I go for this observance. I had a compelling feeling inside me, a feeling of some unseen, unknown need. Little did I realize that the need was to serve Him whom I came to know as the Messiah.

I had heard the babble of the crowds outside the inn where my boys and I were staying. Inns, right in the heart of town, are not like quiet homes surrounded by fertile fields where only the occasional laughter of a child is heard or the braying of an ass. We heard shuffling feet all night long, the clatter of sheep hooves on the pavement early in the morning on the way to market, and the muffled conversations of peasants on the way to some task, religious or commercial. But this babble was different. These were the shouts of indignant people. We were aroused by the commotion and went outside to investigate. Who can subdue bursting curiosity? Especially when he has two excitable young sons with him?

It was a bright, clear morning, but the ugly sounds of the crowd did not match the beauty of the day. Before long we saw Roman soldiers coming, and a man behind them was carrying the *patibulum*, that odious symbol of death and judgment, upon His shoulders. It was a hefty piece of timber, and awkward to handle. The jeering crowd made the load no easier to handle, and the man stumbled near my feet. The timber fell to the stony pavement with a splintering thud. Besides this man (whose name, I soon learned, was Jesus, from Nazareth) there were two others bearing their crosses also, hard-looking, criminal types, who uttered oaths at the unruly crowd.

(Tossing his hands upward) I don't know what they expected of Jesus. After all, He had been scourged at the command of Pontius Pilate, the procurator. He had a crown of spiky branches pressed into His head, and the blood must have obscured His vision as it ran in rivulets from the aching wounds. His robe entangled His feet as it bunched up under His bent frame. How could they expect Him to manage the *patibulum* with all that was wearying Him?

Whether it was compassion for the prisoner, or merely expediency to get the job done and move the prisoners to the place of execution, I don't know, but one of the guards pulled me out of the crowd and made me carry the beam on to Golgotha.

I could have protested, but what is a Jew up against an armed Roman? I thought of my sons, but they were old enough to care for themselves. Perhaps I could have found a worthy excuse, but I could not ignore that poor man's need.

Now I am a fairly strong man. I have done many heavy jobs before, for one cannot supervise his estate well unless he himself puts his shoulder to shove and push, to dig and carry, and get the tasks done. It was not the weight of that heavy load that I feared, but the use to which the Romans intended to put it. What a horrible and merciless method of death! As I bore that cross, I could not help but think of Jesus, who not only had to carry it but would soon be carried by it from life to death, nailed by pounding hammer blows, and lifted up on the upright stake. All the horror of what was happening locked tightly into my mind, and I felt a surging pity for Him. Yet, as I struggled with the beam, *He* seemed to take pity on *me*.

(Simon moves to the center of the chancel; his hands are extended outward in a vague attempt to describe the look.) I cannot adequately describe that look He gave me, that look of compassion and relief, that look of anguish mixed with . . . I guess you would call it hope. There seemed to be an attitude of thanksgiving, of simple yet profound gratitude for the assistance I gave. It was as if He was saying to me that bearing the cross is a necessity, that it was done not alone for Him, and that He would repay my trouble with something more than material things. Was it hope He gave me? He who was soon to die, who was facing the bleakest possible demise, who seemingly had nothing to look forward to but bitter anguish, seemed to give me hope. Was it the assurance that in the face of difficulty He provides strength? I don't know how to word it. All I can say is that I knew that crossbearing is a hard and lonesome task, yet when we look beyond it to the possibilities, we may see hope.

My sons and I were horrified by the brutality of the crucifixion. When we learned that this Jesus was no thief or robber, murderer or insurrectionist, as were the other two and the one they released in His stead, the notorious Barabbas, we could not understand the reason for His death. There seemed to be no justice in it, a mob action, a profaning of the Commandments, and violence against the sanctity of innocent life.

Later I found light in that *patibulum*. I found illumination of my mind. Looking back, that Passover was no longer a celebration of a past event, but once again a very current thing. The Angel of Death was coming again, but this time to strike the firstborn Son of God, so that as the blood of the lamb saved our forebears in Egypt, splashed as it was on their doorposts, the blood of this Lamb would save all our descendants who trusted in Him, splashed as it was on the posts of the cross!

(Sitting down on the top step of the center chancel, Simon

continues to confide what he learned in the Good Friday episode.)

More than crucifixion took place! More than death happened! The wonder of the impossible happened, for Jesus, who died on Friday, was alive again by Sunday morning's first rays of sunlight. I saw Him *die*! One doesn't get a spear thrust into His side and survive very readily. But I also saw Him *after* His miraculous resurrection, and I knew it was truly the One for whom I bore the cross. Those eyes were the same blazing eyes that gave me hope when everything else uttered defeat.

Is that not the beauty of the fulfilled faith we have as Christians? We need not look only at the immediate pain and agony of our crossbearing. We may look toward conquest. We may anticipate victory. No matter how arduous the climb up our own Golgothas, you and I may see light from the cross leading us on to deathless life. Is that not far better than lifeless death?

(Returning to the lectern, Simon continues.) You who grow weary under the burden of the cross of illness, look to Jesus and see hope. You who stumble because of the weighty crosses of family difficulty, take courage in the compassionate understanding of the Lord. You who struggle and sag under the oppressive weight of the cross of uncertainty, know that from the light of the cross of Golgotha you may look beyond the darkness to the Resurrection, to new life.

One may stumble as Jesus did under the weight of the cross imposed upon us, but the Holy Spirit picks us up to help us continue toward our Golgothas assured of victory. Being Christians does not mean we are without trials. We are, however, encouraged to master the moments of anguish because the inspiration of the crossbearing Lord reminds us that every sacrifice under the hand of God may become a satisfaction, a joy of noblest quality. The significance of the cross is not in what it did to Jesus, but in what it did and does for us.

It has taught us to make our burdens blessings, to look for the ways and means by which they may glorify God.

Once in a lifetime we're called out to the streets of life to do something really worthwhile. Many rebel; some walk away from it; and others would rather do almost anything than lift a finger to help Jesus bear His load. I suppose I could have done the same, but I'm glad I didn't. I'm glad that soldier commanded me to serve my Lord. Others who likewise serve Jesus are equally glad they do. So will you if you willingly lift the timbers of heartache and take them to the mount of crucifixion to be executed once and for all, so that out of the grave may arise new life, new hope, new faith.

The cross the Lord carries today is the one of concern for the hungry and uneducated, for the sickly and unwashed millions who are closeted in the backward ghettos of your cities and the backward nations of your continents. Authorities are trying to pull you into service to share the burden. Be receptive to the command to share in bearing this cross, for even if it is a modern "Roman" that calls you to help, it is an invitation from God.

Will you carry it?

Or will you push your way through the crowds seeking a way to escape and miss the greatest opportunity you will have to serve Jesus?

Let us pray. (Standing at the altar, hands upraised, Simon prays.) Jesus, You looked at me and gave me freedom. You were the prisoner and I was the free man, yet You unshackled me from a bondage that I never realized I was in. I took the load of Your cross, yet You bore the weight of my sin. You stumbled, yet I was the one who had fallen. I picked You up and carried Your cross, yet You lifted me up and carried me to eternity. Thank You, Lord, for forcing me to serve. I was the fortunate one, though those around me were momentarily glad they had been passed by.

Now take these Your servants here and empower them to carry their crosses to the place of resolution, remembering that crucifixion is a painful process but the only way to resurrection. Help us to look beyond the pain to the pleasure of achievement.

Through Your Spirit help us not to think that the little crosses of straw we bear compare with the magnitude of the cross You carried. Instead, inspire us by Your crossbearing to see that we too may lift heavy loads and thereby glorify You. Thank You, Jesus. Amen.

MALCHUS

Malchus requires no particular setting. You may wish him to stand at a lectern closer to the congregation, in the lower chancel.

He is a rather lackluster person, that is, aside from the incident with Peter we would probably never have known of him. Thus his appearance is not startling or particularly colorful, but rather bland. It is his message and witness that adds sparkle.

Costumed, Malchus might wear a short tunic with sandals and a cloak about his shoulders with a typical head *kaffiyeh*. A cord is worn in place of a sash.

Modern dress might include jeans, turtleneck and cap, something that might be worn almost anywhere most of the year-round.

This version of Malchus is played with jargon and street dialect. Let him be as earthy as possible without achieving a "Deadend Kid" image that overwhelms the message.

Note that an acolyte brings out a lectern at the proper time, and also whispers in his ear when requested for the "hearing test."

The text for this service might be John 18:1-11.

Note: The enterprising congregation attempting to stimulate family attendance at midweek services might use this device for Malchus: Make a large batch of "Malchus ears," sugar cookies, to be taken home for a bedtime snack. They can be packaged in sandwich bags. They're easily made by using a heart-shaped cookie cutter and cutting the hearts down the middle. By flipping one side over you'll have plenty of "right ears" to share with the kids as an object lesson, a reminder of the one who lost an ear to Peter but gained hearing from Jesus.

MALCHUS

Ooee! (Malchus looks around at the church and is impressed by its beauty and the people present.) I had no idea there was to be a crowd here. I ain't no speaker. You best be gettin' someone who can get his verbs unmixed with his nouns. Anyhow, I ain't nobody. My name means little to most, save my old Maw.

The name's Malchus . . . M-a-l-k-u-z! Ever hear anybody else with a name like that? Course not! It's one of those funny ones that sweet little babies get stuck with, and when they're big enough to change it, the name's too ingrained to get rid of it.

Where you want me to stand? Up there? (He points to the pulpit.) I ain't no speaker, but I'm gonna have to lean on something. My legs is aquiverin' as though they was made of boiled figs. (An acolyte brings a small lectern to the center of the chancel.)

Now I know why you want me here, and I'll try to make it as painless as I can. I'll just tell it like it was, and you can take it from there. Now, let's see, where was I? (Remembering)

If none of you have heard of me, I don't blame you none. I had one little brush with fame, and though it didn't start out right, it wound up mighty fine. It all happened so fast that it's amazin' I should be remembered at all.

I'm ashamed to confess that I came with the soldiers and the crowd that was following Judas to a little garden outside Jerusalem. They was goin' to arrest Jesus, that Galilean rabbi who had my master, the high priest, all unglued. Nothin' very excitin' ever happens where I am, so when that came up, I thought to myself, this is gonna be worth watchin', so I tagged along.

As far as I know, that Jesus fellow hadn't done nothin' that deserved jail, but then the Romans never made no practice of tellin' me what they were up to, or who they suspected of insurrection or sabotage. The high priest neither. He didn't care for no man, least of all his bonded servants. I was no more to him than just another slave to clean up after him. I did my job and kept my nose clean. I had enough beatin's and mistreatment to keep from invitin' more of the same.

Frankly, I didn't give much thought to the shifty goin's-on in the high priest's palace. You'd think a man of religion like himself would have the decency to want justice, but not his nibs. I felt they knew what they was doin', and I wanted to see their little plots carried out just for the sake of some excitement.

The fact is, I never took sides. I just watched life pass by. I wasn't fond of the high priest and I wasn't a follower of Jesus, so it didn't make no difference to me who got hurt, as long as it wasn't me. Them big names made the world go round, and I just looked on. They had the names, and all I had were some hopes that the evening wouldn't be as boring as most of them were.

I was young, and I liked adventure. It wasn't what they call *high* adventure, and it never got very far out of the gutter, but it gave the old ticker a little juice for sputtering along. There wasn't too much that happened in Jerusalem that I didn't see, but always from a safe distance, understand? I ain't one of these characters that looks for a fight, or a trouble-starter. I just like to watch the action, but back a few feet, you know what I mean?

But this time, in the pitch-dark night, when all we had was a few lanterns to find our way through the olive trees, I wasn't as careful as I shoulda been.

I lost an ear.

Yep, I lost an ear. Can you imagine? (Confiding in the great-storyteller style) There we was, a detail of soldiers and a group of followers of the Pharisees, and some of us from the household of Caiaphas. Judas from Kerioth, near the Dead Sea, was aleadin' us, 'cause he had been one of the rabbi's followers. He took us to the Garden of Gethsemane on the slope of the Mount of Olives. Jesus often went there, he'd said, and sometimes His followers came too. Some of our gang carried torches, and so we looked like a mob about to stir up the dust of Jerusalem.

When we came to Jesus and three of His disciples, it was easy to see even in that dim light that all He was doin' was prayin', and the disciples asleepin'. They yawned and rubbed their eyes like they must have really been zonked. The big one, he was known as Peter. Someone said the other two were fishermen from Galilee, James and John. But they was outnumbered and they was doin' all they could to play it cool.

Old Judas just waltzed himself right up to Jesus and planted a kiss right on Him. It wasn't no way for a friend to act, if you ask me. He was really betrayin' Jesus with a kiss, but I ain't sure that Judas thought of it that way. I have the feelin' that he thought what he was doin' was somethin' noble, trying to get Jesus to start some kind of riot or revolution. If that's what it was, it didn't work.

(Leans forward on the lectern.) It was Jesus who asked kinda polite like, "Whom do you seek?" The mob let Him know: "Jesus of Nazareth."

"I am He," He said softly. He said it in such a way that the crowd drew back and fell to the ground. I don't know what they were thinkin'. Maybe they expected Him to send lightning bolts from His fingertips. He asked them again who they were looking for, and they answered a second time, "Jesus of Nazareth."

In a stronger voice, He said this time, "I told you that I am He; so, if you seek Me, let these men go." Can you imagine that? He wanted to have no company in His agony. If it was me, I'd have gotten the whole bunch to go along to the pokey, but He defended His friends.

Then that monster of a fisherman attacked. Peter lunged into the crowd with his sword drawn, and before I knew what was ahappenin' he sliced off my right ear as neatly as if I'd been a sausage fresh out of the springhouse.

But Jesus said, "No more of this!"

I guess I was in shock, but before I realized what was takin' place I felt the warmth of His hand, and before I could figure it all out I was healed. My ear was just like it was before, and my hearing was sharp as ever.

(He motions to the acolyte who brought out the lectern to come over to him. It's to be a hearing test.)

Whisper in my ear, son. Go ahead. Whisper softly. (It's done.)

The lad here whispered in my right ear, "Cookies and milk if you hurry up!" Sounds like somethin' to eat, so I'll make it quick. But you can see my ear is as good as new. Jesus healed it.

I was almost sick inside; sick because I realized that this man was no criminal. It made me sick that my masters should plot against someone who spent His life healing people, who even healed me, one of the mob that was out to get Him. I had heard the stories of His fantastic healings, but they didn't mean nothin' at all to me until He touched my cut-off ear and made it well.

It was as if He cured my blindness too. Now I wasn't really

blind, you see, but I wasn't seein' very well either. I saw lots of dirty tricks goin' on and I never said nothin', like I was blind and without a voice as well as minus a pair of ears. But that touch of His seemed to wake me up and start me on a new life. My mind began to tick off all I'd heard, and somehow that brain of mine began clicking out things I'd never thought much about before. Like: Why was everybody so fired up about makin' sacrifices at the temple to atone for sin, when they didn't often follow it up with a little kindness of their own? Or like: Why was this high priest so put out because Jesus chased them rascals out of the temple who were cheatin' all the worshipers? You should be able to go into the temple and expect honest men to deal honestly with you. Well, all sorts of things started jarrin' inside my head. I kept thinkin' about myself. Here I was accusin' others with not doin' what they said they believed. I wasn't neither.

Bet you have that trouble now and then too, don'tcha?

That touch of Jesus seemed to shake some sense into me.

The guards and officers grabbed Jesus and tied Him up real good. There wasn't no need for that, and they knew it, but they weren't goin' to take no chances. They tied them holy hands as if He was a cheap criminal, a common thief.

I couldn't believe they hadn't seen what He did to me, yet they ignored it like it was nothin'. Didn't they hear my scream when Peter's blade came down against my head and sliced off my ear? Didn't they see Jesus touch my ear and leave me without a scar?

They were blind, and it wasn't the fault of the dark night. It was the darkness in their hearts. It was as if I myself had been washed by the brightest moonlight ever. I wasn't nobody, but Jesus didn't check my credentials before He cured me. For the first time my ears were opened to hear love. Caiaphas had never spoken a kind word to me in all the years I served him, nor had Annas.

Yet I couldn't feel no anger toward them, only pity.

They was the ones who plotted against Jesus and said that "one man should die for the people."

I later went to see two of the disciples that were with Jesus. I wanted to talk to them about this rabbi. I was pretty scared, but I wasn't gonna forget what He'd done for me. I had to learn more about that man who restored my ear.

I spent the night just thinkin'. I was stunned by what my friends told me about Him. They talked about miracles and

Lazarus comin' to life after bein' dead for four days. They told me about His message, about God's love. I never knew God loved anybody, but Jesus said so. In fact, God so loved me that I got to meet His only Son, and now I know what it means to be really forgiven.

How's your hearin'? Are you hearin' what I'm saying'? I know some of you young people think this is just a lot of nonsense. Well, that's because you're young and you haven't got into the prophets to hear what they said about the Messiah, but if you'll listen to Malchus, you'll see that the Bible tells the truth. I know some of you older people think that because everything's goin' your way God doesn't really matter unless there's an earthquake or drought or somethin'. But I say He does matter. He matters every day, in little things and in big ones too. If you don't believe that, well, I guess you're worse off than me when I had my right ear cut off. You ain't hearin' so good yourself.

But listen, God is speakin' right now.

He wants you to clean out of your mind all that clutter that don't mean nothin' and start hearin' the good news Jesus has for you. He wants to chase out everythin' that's ugly in your life and fill it with sunshine. He wants to stuff you with His love so that you won't be such an old grouch with the kids or with the neighbors. He wants you to know that nothin' stands in your way of goin' to the top, of bein' good at whatever you want to be, as you let Him heal your hearin' and seein' and thinkin' and bein'.

Well, that night was so long and so full of thinkin' for me that I wanted to go out and rescue Jesus. Can you figure it? *I* wanted to rescue *Him*—single-handed. But then I started thinkin': It wasn't I that needed to rescue Him, but it was He that rescued me in that garden. He didn't need my help. Later I realized that by dying on the cross and rising from the tomb He rescued me again—this time from everlasting death. He saved me!

He wants to save you too!

Let Him.

Let Him make you God's child through Baptism. Let Him get into your brain so that you start thinkin' about important stuff instead of nail polish and ball games. Now, that don't mean little things ain't important. If they're important to us, they're important to God too. But He wants us to see that there are some mighty important things that get shelved when all we think about is our next adventure. That's the way my life used to be.

Jesus showed me somethin' much more important. He showed me love; and when you've experienced that, then nothin' else is even close.

When Jesus restored my ear, I heard His message of love, and it never left me. I ain't very good at talkin' about it in public, but then I don't have to be a great speaker. It's not just somethin' to talk about. It's somethin' to live and do and be.

Hey, it's been great sharin' with you.

See this dagger? (He displays a knife.) It means death—that's why people carry daggers. You know what it means to me? It means life. When I see it, I think of Peter's sword; and if Peter hadn't cut off my ear, I never would have heard the Gospel of Jesus nor learned that there's more to living than just lookin' for adventure. There's enjoyin' the adventure God gives to everybody who believes in Jesus—the adventure of forever. (He exits down the center aisle, shaking hands with people along the way, greeting them with "shalom.")

CENTURION

This character is a commanding presence. After all, he was a commander of men, and he possesses a military bearing that is unmistakable. He often stands with hands on hips, legs wide apart, chest erect, looking directly at his audience as General Patton may have gazed at his troops on the drill field.

An old surplice serves well as a Roman tunic. Draw it together at the waist with a white cord. A brightly colored cloak (red or orange) is pinned to each shoulder and allowed to fall so that it drapes in a "u" shape on the back. Use regimental or company crests (that most former G.I.'s still have) to pin the cloak.

A military overskirt may be made of tan fabric. Cut the overskirt so that it looks like a picket fence upside down, with the "pickets" remaining together at the waistband. To add to the military appearance of the overskirt, staple cardboard covered with foil to the tip of each "picket." Gold- or copper-colored foil looks best. He needs no sword or shield or helmet, unless these are available to you. A shield could be used as well as a camp stool and "campaign desk" from someone's bedroom furniture to add atmosphere for the portrayal.

A former serviceman who still fits his uniform may be willing to don it for a contemporary dress portrayal.

The text for this service might be Luke 23:44-49.

CENTURION

(The Centurion rises, goes to greet an unseen guest, and shows him into the room.)

Please come in and be seated, my friend. Take that couch there (pointing). I believe you will be more comfortable. You say you have just come from the port at Ostia? You have come all the way from Ptolemais of Phoenicia, you say? That's a long journey by sea. It requires at least a week to recover from such a voyage. How grateful I am to the gods that I never entered the navy!

Yes, it is true that I once served in the imperial army. Those were exciting days indeed. Whereas I enjoy my retirement here in the country, the peace and the quiet is a little too much for me at times. I often long for the glamour of visiting far-off places, but spare me the ships. I would rather march, ride a horse, or travel on foot.

As a soldier I served throughout the empire. From Rome to Neapolis, back to Brundisium, and on again to Leontopolis in Egypt before finally being assigned to duty in Palestine.

I moved up through the ranks to become a centurion, a commander of a hundred men. To keep a hundred wifeless men in check takes more than courage, dear Luke. It requires blatant ignorance! (He laughs at his own joke.)

We were stationed with the imperial garrison at Caesarea, and it was from there that I was finally sent home to the olive groves of Latium. Ever since, I've been supervising my family's holdings and commanding my slaves as if they were infantrymen (said with humor). It's not as rigorous as the life of a soldier, but to hear my slaves complain you would think we were Caesar's elite guard.

It isn't that our acreage is large, but this farm and these buildings have been in our family for many generations. I would have liked to continue traveling to the exotic cities of the Orient and Africa to maintain Roman peace and order, but family demands were too great for me to continue my wanderlust.

Yes, my friend, I'm reasonably happy here. We are only a few miles north of Rome. Get on the Via Latina, and we are there within hours, if we desire metropolitan excitement. If we want the cooling breezes of the Tyrrhenian Sea when summer heat makes even the olive trees seem to wither, we head for the beach a few miles to the west. It's a lovely region here, and my wife and children and I enjoy the contemplative life.

But you said you have a particular interest in my days in Jerusalem, didn't you? I believe you said you are a physician, eh Luke? That is your name? I believe that's Greek rather than Hebrew; correct me if you will.

This narrative you are writing, it's about Jesus the Nazarene prophet, I see. (Suspiciously) Are *you* a followers of the Way?

I've heard a great deal about that Messianic sect of the Jews, even here in Rome. News travels quickly, and Pontius Pilate himself returned here to the contempt of the emperor.

Fortunately, I did not have to serve on his administrative staff, nor can anyone accuse me of being sympathetic with Pilate's brand of Roman justice. I, too, could have been touched by the scandals surrounding him, so you can see my gratitude that I had *other* duties.

Although my company and I were stationed for the most part in Caesarea, on the Mediterranean coast of Israel, we would quite often make the march to Jerusalem, to the fortress of Antonia. You know that it was named after Mark Anthony, don't you? He's one Roman soldier who made the world his backyard.

The Jews are a curious lot. Unlike us Romans and Greeks, they believe in only *one* God. I thought them spiritually bankrupt at first. Instead of our interminable shrines and our innumerable holidays, they have but *one* temple, in Jerusalem, and a few feasts that they observe. If not bankrupt, they seemed shortchanged by our standards.

Let me see, their new year begins in autumn, as I recall, and they celebrate another major commemoration in the spring. They call it Passover. It recalls their escape (fumbling for almost forgotten facts) from Egypt, and the beginning of the 40-year-long wandering in the wilderness before they drove the Canaanites out from the land they claim God promised them.

They had several exceptional generals, you know. They were not always a conquered people, enslaved to some mightier power. One general was named Joshua. We have long admired him, and David too, one of their kings. He was a crafty military tactician.

We have often studied his battle strategy. (Laughing) Even the Jews had their military geniuses.

But back to the story I began. You will have to forgive me for wandering at times. One event triggers another in my mind, and each was so monumentally impressive that I have not easily forgotten anything that occurred during those days I was a commander in Palestine.

We were indeed concerned that the Jews would try to revolt. They were an obstinate people, with much pride, and an arrogant demeanor that few of us could stomach. That intrigued me, however, rather than revolted me, strange as it may sound. I was at first affronted by their haughtiness, but the more I observed, the more I was aware that here was a spiritual pride and unique cultural loyalty that I had not seen before, neither in Egypt, nor Greece, and not even in gloriously beautiful Italy.

I became convinced that it had a great deal to do with their religious faith, and so I spent considerable time studying their peculiarities, even to the point of living for a time as they do. As I said, I was intrigued (chuckling, though serious). I wondered what would cause a man to live as they do, to believe as they believed, to be so deeply loyal to a seemingly lost cause as they were, and so I emulated them, but only briefly. Their dietary laws were too strict. Can you imagine *never* eating pork, and me a hog raiser, and having to comply with all their fussy regulations? It was worse than the army. For me it was a thrust into pious severity that I found interesting for a time, but I grew weary of it. It was not a discipline that I found exacted the best in a person.

I must say, however, that philosophically there was far more substance to their beliefs than to our myths or to our practice of them. There was a holiness in their Scriptures which we cannot find among the gods and goddesses of the Roman Pantheon, or Mount Olympus for that matter, Luke.

The Jews were an exclusive and elusive people. They forbade non-Jews to enter their temple, and even their synagogs were sanctuaries that few Romans visited.

(The Centurion rises, stretches his arms and legs, and stands with hands on hips.)

They had a belief that their God would one day send what they called (searching for the right word) a "Messiah," a kind of Savior, Redeemer, one who would rescue them from their predicaments and make their nation great again. To tell you the truth, Dr. Luke, I really thought it was some of their positive thinking, some peculiar Oriental strategy to put psychological fear into their enemies. They believed the idea fiercely, of course. Every now and then they thought their Messiah had come. Some political fanatic would gain their attention, or some alleged wonder worker or zealous rabbi from the hills would stir up the people. We put more than one in prison, and a host of them met death by crucifixion or the sword.

There is one in particular that I recall most vividly, for He seemed different from the rest. He seemed far and away above all the others. He was not arrogant, but He had a quality I can't begin to describe. He had an enigmatic smile, a charisma that charmed the throngs—except those that cried for His murder. His eyes were piercing, penetrating, and yet there was warmth to be felt in His gaze akin to none other. They said He was from Nazareth in northern Galilee. He is the very one you have called Jesus the Christ.

He had quite a reputation. Another centurion told me that Jesus healed his ailing servant. He was from Capernaum on the north shore of the Sea of Tiberias in Galilee. There were other fantastic tales about His healing powers. Some said He had fed thousands with a few fish and several loaves of bread, and that the amount left over was far more than they began with. He could command the stormy waters on the lake to subside, they reported, and they went so far as to claim that He had actually called a man from Bethany to life again. They told other stories about the message He preached. There was no call for violence in either His preaching or healing, and He didn't seem concerned about extorting money from the ignorant or gaining office, like so many opportunists. He did upset the temple authorities when He drove out the money changers one day. He said the temple was to be a holy place, and they had made it a nest of thievery. He was undoubtedly correct. There was little charity among those religionists. They liked their gold and their power, and by using their own temple money they could fool the poor pilgrims who came from out of town and didn't know what the proper exchange was.

He was not well received by the "religious" authorities, yet He was a fervent, practicing Jew. I don't know what they disliked about Him, except that He never yielded to their trickery. He even called them "whited sepulchres," and you know how Jews regard a dead body! The Pharisees and the Sanhedrin and the chief priests arranged for Jesus to be arrested, paying one of that man's own disciples to betray Him, after which the Nazarene was eventually crucified.

I was commander of the detail at the Antonia fortress when they brought Him to Pilate to be judged. My men had their fun with the prisoner. It made me sick, but they tell me it's good for the men's morale.

All along, Jesus looked at us with such compassion that I was stirred within. It became more and more another miscarriage of justice in my mind, but then I silenced myself with a command to obey, to do my duty, to put foolishness out of my head. It was none of my affair, after all. I was not to judge the Galilean, or Pilate for his indiscretion either. I had a job to do, and I did it, but when He stumbled carrying the cross I did get another Jew to finish carrying it to the top of Golgotha. As they drove those spikes into His flesh I cringed within. He had done nothing that was against either the law of the Jews or the law of the Romans as far as I could tell. He happened to be disliked by a powerful few, and they were having their revenge. I didn't think such a thing could happen in this modern day. I was revolted. Pilate was a weakling, and because of his moral ineptness my company and I had to do his dirty work.

I spoke with one of Jesus' followers, a man named John. He had been a fisherman in Galilee before he took up the Nazarene's teachings as his own. He talked about forgiveness for sins, and that God desires reconciliation with mankind. (Wistfully) I really wish I could believe that myself! He said the Nazarene's Father is God, and that His mission is to draw sinners into fellowship with Him. I couldn't grasp all that John said, but he kept talking about prophecy being fulfilled, whatever that referred to. I couldn't remember all the Jewish Scriptures I had read.

There were two robbers with Jesus when He was crucified. And there was quite a mob, quite a crowd that gathered. Strange how something so brutal brings out the worst in people. The curious and the bloodthirsty, they all came. My men had to keep pushing the Pharisees and their adherents back. They jeered at Jesus with circus humor. (Mockingly) "He saved others; He cannot save Himself. Let the Christ, the King of Israel, come down from the cross," "that we may see and believe." Believe? Ha! Even the robbers reviled Him, yet one spoke up in defense of

Jesus, and from the cross the Nazarene promised him Paradise.

Jesus almost had me sold on His holiness. He prayed aloud: "Father, forgive them; for they know not what they do." I heard every word that man said from the cross. The more I heard, the more I was forced to reflect upon what I had learned as I studied the Jewish Scriptures. If He was not the Messiah, there was an awesome sacredness in every word He spoke that jarred me.

At noon the sky was blackened with the most dismal clouds I've ever seen. It was dark as night, and everyone became afraid. I heard Jesus cry with a loud voice some garbled words. Then I realized it was Hebrew. John said Jesus was quoting the words of an old Hebrew song: "My God, My God, why hast Thou forsaken Me?" He told me they were not words of defeat, but of deepest agony. I could not understand that! Some thought Jesus was calling to one of the ancient prophets of Judaism to come and rescue Him. They wanted to watch and see if Elijah would come. One of the Jewish assistants rushed to Him with a sponge of sour wine to aid Him in His agony, but he was told to wait and see whether or not Elijah was going to rescue Him.

Then He breathed His last, and at that instant it was as if the whole earth was shuddering from grief. There was a quake that caused fissures in the ground, one that zigzagged across Calvary from the cross to the Pharisees themselves, like the accusing finger of God. You should have heard them cry in fear! Later someone came running to say that the temple curtain covering their Most Holy Place was ripped from top to bottom by the tremor.

Whether it was my fright, or whether all the facts of my studies of Judaism and my encounter with Jesus were finally merging into some sort of faith, I don't know, but I exclaimed with a heart of anguish to those murderous religionists: "Truly this man was the Son of God!" "Certainly this man was innocent!" I said to them, and they felt the sting of my rebuke. Many of them left in fear and some in sorrow, beating their breasts.

One of my guards took his lance and pierced Jesus' side to assure that His death was complete. We weren't going to have any make-believe. A wealthy man from the little town of Arimathea near the Samaritan border, Joseph I think was his name, asked for the lifeless body. He and Nicodemus wanted to bury Him. Dusk was coming soon, and since it was the Jewish sabbath of Passover, they had to hasten to get Him to the tomb before sundown. It was a gruesome Friday, that one, a horrible prelude to the Passover feast.

Later my men took the watches guarding the tomb. And it was my "brave" (said mockingly) men who were dazzled by the appearance of what they said were angels, and discovered the sealed entrance to the tomb had been rolled open and the body was gone. They were scared blue. That was the third day since the crucifixion, and the guards were paid off not to talk about it. It was rumored that Jesus had risen from the dead. I suppose that's the reason Pilate hastened my orders, for we were ordered to leave immediately for Caesarea, and another detachment was sent to relieve us. The high priest had intimidated Pilate once again.

We marched to Caesarea that very night, and it wasn't long before I was sent back to Italy, a captain mind you, with exemplary citations, to report to the military commandant. Eventually I received honorable retirement with a generous pension from Rome. But Dr. Luke, I've never forgotten what took place there in Jerusalem. I often think of it yet.

As a matter of fact, I just received a letter from my cousin Cornelius, who is still stationed in Caesarea. He's also a centurion. He wrote about discovering something wonderful that he wants to share with the whole family. He referred to those perplexing days in Jerusalem and said that it was all true—Jesus was, and is, really the Messiah. Someone by the name of Peter, I believe it was, talked with Cornelius about the Gospel of Jesus, and he accepted it. Cornelius is too bright to be easily hoodwinked, too careful to be carried away by some fanciful philosophy. Say, wasn't Peter the disciple who was there when Jesus was judged and denied knowing Him?

Cornelius wrote about being baptized. That's a Jewish rite for converts, isn't it, Dr. Luke? Do Jesus-ites practice baptism also? There are many questions coming to my mind that I want to ask you, good friend. You say you are composing this narrative for a friend named Theophilus? Why not share some of your investigative reporting with me? Why not give this old Roman the benefit of your harvest of knowledge? I'm sure Theophilus won't mind. I am, I hesitate to admit, interested, even sympathetic to the Way!

Enjoy my hospitality, Dr. Luke. (Rising) Let's go into the

atrium. I'll introduce you to my family; they too will want to hear the stories you have to tell about Jesus the Christ.

(Stretching) It seems like yesterday that I stood on the skull-shaped hill of Calvary. Come, Luke, let's adjourn to the courtyard for our meal, and then we must talk of lofty things again, of this Gospel Cornelius writes about.

There's a bit of a void within this soul that needs some help. Perhaps a physician like you will have the right medicine to correct it. Come. (He exits.)

NICODEMUS

Nicodemus is an older man. His hair may be grayed with corn starch or a rinse, if desired. He wears a full-length tunic and a dark cloak over it with sandals and a *kaffiyeh* (desert headdress).

To add an interesting dimension to the portrayal of Nicodemus, play him with a crackling voice that suggests age.

A business suit would be fine for modern-dress presentation, but a subdued color with equally dark tie is preferred. Nicodemus is more the conservative leader than the *avant garde* Middle Easterner. Perhaps a black felt hat could be worn, as seen in synagogs today, or a *yarmulke*, a skullcap.

Nicodemus may be seated on a chair near a table with a candle on it to suggest the darkness of the night he visited the Lord. Dim the church lights.

If you wish to give the children a little memento of Nicodemus, consider a luminous cross. They are available at modest cost and remind children of the man who came by night and discovered the Light of hope. A candlelight service ending is also appropriate.

The text for this service might be John 3:1-21.

NICODEMUS

(Standing up, Nicodemus is reflecting on the past, pensive.)

How much the still darkness reminds me of that night when I sought out Jesus. I had to have answers to my questions. It was like a plaguing itch that couldn't be scratched. I had to know who He was, and be assured that I had made no mistake in my admiration for Him. One does well to be cautious in such matters. One dare not go after a whisp of smoke thinking it to be a ladder to the seventh heaven. One tests and checks and studies and prays.

Scoundrels had come before claiming to be the Messiah. I could not afford to make so serious an error in judgment. One must consider his reputation, the standing of his family. Yet how unimportant these things are if one were really to find that it is no fraud, but the Messiah in the flesh! It was necessary to be quite certain that this Jesus from Nazareth in Galilee was no ordinary man. One may call it stealth, but I prefer to think of it as wisdom. I went under cover of darkness through the rambling streets of Jerusalem to confront the rabbi Jesus with my questions.

I suppose I rightly deserve the title "timid," awarded me by many because I hid behind the anonymity of darkness. Some have even named me the "Night Disciple" (chuckling knowingly to himself), but it was out of that inky darkness that I found the Light of life. . . . As a rabbi myself, one of the members of the ruling rabbinical body, the Sanhedrin, I did not wish to give my support, tacit or otherwise, unless I had assurances of His genuineness. One does not give up his lifelong methods of research to follow only his emotions in such an instance. Because a man is old doesn't mean he must play the fool.

But let me tell you what I found. (He settles down into the chair.)

I told Him as honestly as I could my respect for His ministry. "Rabbi," I said to Jesus, "we know that You are a teacher come from God; for no one can do these signs that You do, unless God is with him."

I had heard His preaching, His exceptional understanding of Scriptural passages, as well as His sensitivity to God as a loving Father, and I had seen the clear evidence of His marvelous power. There was every reason for the most cautious scholar to believe that here was truly a prophet of the Most High God.

Then Jesus startled me by saying a most puzzling thing: "Unless one is born anew, he cannot see the kingdom of God."

Now, it is not difficult to comprehend one's physical birth, but two births is quite another matter! I did not know whether He was making a fool of me or whether I was drained of my intellect. I asked: "How can a man be born when he is old? Can he enter a second time into his mother's womb and be born?" These were not such silly questions, my friends, for the rabbi Jesus was not known to jest flippantly; therefore He would react to my questions with seriousness.

His response was almost as enigmatic as the initial one. "Unless one is born of water and the Spirit, he cannot enter the kingdom of God. That which is born of the flesh is flesh," He said, "and that which is born of the Spirit is spirit."

To you who know the delights of Christian baptism, such words have little mystery. You know what they imply, but I was not so privileged. It was a conundrum. I had had a fine education, sitting at the feet of the most profound scholars of the time, but aside from the ceremonial baptism of cleansing as a sign of renewal, I had not met the miracle wrought by the sacrament Jesus instituted. I did not know that Baptism is a second birth, that it is being born again.

Jesus sensed my puzzlement, however, and sought to clear up my confusion. "Do not marvel that I said to you, 'You must be born anew,'" He said. "The wind blows where it wills, and you hear the sound of it, but you do not know whence it comes or whither it goes; so it is with every one who is born of the Spirit."

I inquired again how this could be, and He explained to me with infinite patience that despite my lavish training in the intellectual and theological disciplines of our people, I had missed the mystery of God's might that is able to accomplish what a man is incapable of fulfilling. God is God, and despite the wisdom of the *Midrash* and the *Talmud*, He alone determines the means by which man is saved. Even the most faithful give in to doubt at times, as evidenced by Jonah and the Lord's disciples. Jesus graciously reached out to strengthen my weak knowledge and inspire faith.

I do not know how the wind blows, but that it blows! I know that it truly blows, for I see the leaves waver and I hear them rustle; yet I cannot see the wind, nor can I box it as I can fruit from the orchard or bottle it like wine from grapes. The wind, so simple a thing, yet so grand that it is an inexplicable mystery, helps us to comprehend what it means to be "born anew." Via water and the Spirit, via the action of God and the use of water, man has his second birth! It is a spiritual rebirth, as the first was physical.

It was in this conversation with the rabbi Jesus that He gave me another clue to the mystery of His Gospel that I would not comprehend for some time to come. He told me: "As Moses lifted up the serpent in the wilderness, so must the Son of man be lifted up, that whoever believes in Him may have eternal life." Remember, Moses put the serpent on a pole so that those who looked at it might be saved from death. Jesus Himself was raised on the cross, so that those who look to Him in faith might have salvation.

He went on to explain to me how "God so loved the world that He gave His only Son, that whoever believes in Him should not perish but have eternal life. For God sent the Son into the world, not to condemn the world, but that the world might be saved through Him."

I came out of the dark night into the glorious light of truth. Jesus became my Light to eternity. He went on to say: "This is the judgment, that the light has come into the world, and men loved darkness rather than light, because their deeds were evil." It's true. It's true "that every one who does evil hates the light, and does not come to the light, lest his deeds should be exposed." It's also true that "He who does what is true comes to the light, that it may be clearly seen that his deeds have been wrought in God." So the burglar loves darkness, as does the murderer. In Jesus we have light.

Baptism means light for those of us lost in the darkness of spiritual ignorance. It means God has focused His Son-ray upon us so that we may see our way out of the quagmires of sin, down the treacherous, robber-hidden highways into eternity. One small flame may guide the lost in the bleakest night. Have you never found yourself out in the lonely country late at night, unsure of your bearings, until you see a dim light off in the distance and it tells you where you are? Jesus became that kind of light to me, the one who sought Him out in the dark night. He became a light that comforted me and gave hope to my despair.

The wolf and the lion stalk the darkness, but the sheep treasure the sunlight as a friend.

Jesus is our Light. That was my experience. It's what gave me courage to speak up and defend Him before the Sanhedrin when they sought to kill Him. (Rises, moves toward the congregation.) "Does our law judge a man without first giving him a hearing and learning what he does?" I asked. I was rebuked for that logical question! They told me that no prophecy foretold the coming of a prophet, not to mention the Messiah, from Galilee.

They did not know, nor did I at the time, that He was born in Judea, in David's town, as the prophet Micah had foretold.

I tried to maneuver behind the scenes to release Him. I spoke to my friend Joseph, the Arimathean, and together we did our best to persuade the seventy priests, scribes, and elders in the Sanhedrin to change their minds. But Annas and Caiaphas had blinded their eyes, and they would not transgress the will of the chief priests. Even the learned can be stupid, as I myself know!

Jesus had brought me out of the utter darkness of fear and uncertainty to know the abundant love of God. He brought peace to my heart. He gave life to my old bones and put light into my heart so that I would never be in darkness again . . . (with pathos) yet I could not save Him; only He could save me!

In my sorrow after His death I realized what He meant by what He had told me that night, and how the mystery of new birth in Baptism and faith brings about new life. I knew He had saved me.

All that Joseph and I could do was to claim His lifeless body. I didn't care what the rest of the rabbis had to say about it—and they said plenty. My fellow Pharisees whispered about our *unusual* interest in the Nazarene, as if it were some exorbitant heresy, some spiritual *faux pas*, but my grief over their frenzied gossip could not dislodge this one last thing I could do for my Lord. Joseph had a tomb, recently cut into the stone wall of a nearby cliff, with a pleasant little garden before it. It was but a few hundred feet from Golgotha, the Place of the Skull, where Jesus had been crucified. We claimed His tortured body and entombed it, wrapping it gently with linen cloths in which we tucked spices to preserve the flesh. I had brought a hundred pounds of aloes and myrrh for the painful, sorrowful task of embalming.

Isn't it strange that at His coming into the world the Wise Men from the East also brought myrrh, as if they knew what would befall the King born in Bethlehem's stable?

The gravestone was rolled over the doorway and sealed by the guards, and Joseph and I trudged the sorrowful journey home.

Then on the third day I heard the marvelous news that He had risen. Now I was rid of all doubt and questioning. I was born anew.

You, too, must be born anew. In the water of Baptism the Spirit gives us new birth, but sometimes, sometimes one is not aware what the Spirit has given to him until he searches for it and uncovers it by a faith that claims the mystery, understood or not, the good news in Christ.

Surreptitiously in our minds we prowl around in the darkness of ignorance, making assumptions about God that are without fact or reason, doubting Him, ignoring Him, brutalizing our concept of deity by unfamiliarity with Him. But there is light in the Word of God, light that shows us Jesus, light that brightens our darkened minds and floods our inner beings with joy.

Come out of the darkness, my friends. Come into the light. I went by night to meet a rabbi and instead encountered my soul. I went in the murky gloom of late evening and discovered light to foster my hopes and comfort my yearnings. I found the Christ of God. I went to straighten out my puzzled mind and found my heart was warmed and brightened.

(Rises, with the candleholder in his hand.)

I shall never fear the world knowing my allegiance to Him. And you? Are you still cowering in the shadows of night, afraid to tell the world that Jesus is the Messiah, your Lord, our Savior?

Come out of the darkness. We need no more "Night Disciples," backing off into the bleakness again. Jesus is the Light of lights . . . let Him enlighten and enliven you.

Shalom, good friends.

(Here Nicodemus may take his candle and extend the light to those along the center aisle to be passed along their rows for a service of light in a darkened church. Such hymns as "Thy Strong Word Did Cleave the Darkness," "Lord Jesus Christ, My

Life, My Light," or "Light of the Anxious Heart" may be sung by a soloist, choir, or the congregation.

A concluding prayer may be:

Light of light, eternal Lord, we come in the darkness of our uncertainty to discover the brightness of Your love. We come to share our doubts so that You may illuminate our shaded thoughts with wisdom, providing us insight into the mysteries that seem so dense and frightening, correcting our gloom with the bloom of Your love. As Nicodemus came in the midnight of fear, encourage us to come to You with our concerns. As he stood before the world of his peers to question their brutal plans, so challenge us to stand even taller before our brothers and sisters to point to the Light. As he cared for You in laying Your body to rest, enable us by the power of Your Spirit to care for those who are spiritually dying and need the myrrh of kindliness and the aloes of insistence, for Your body today is the church we love. Then sprinkle our minds, as we have been baptized, with that assurance of conviction that enables us to be born anew day after day by repentance and faith so we can live as little lights in a darkened world. All this we ask in Your name who are Light and Life and Power. Amen.